CONTEMPORARY
MILLINERY

CONTEMPORARY MILLINERY

HAT DESIGN AND CONSTRUCTION

sophie beale

SCHIFFER PUBLISHING

4880 Lower Valley Road • Atglen, PA 19310

For
Fin, Vincent & Vivienne

Special thanks to Steve & Jo at BlueRed Press
for planting the seed and ensuring it grew

Other Schiffer Books on Related Subjects:
1,000 Hats, Norma Shephard, ISBN 978-0-7643-2403-1
Macramé Couture, Gwenaël Petiot, ISBN 978-0-7643-5991-0
Artisan Felting, Jenny Hill, ISBN 978-0-7643-5852-4

Library of Congress Control Number: 2021942730

Produced by BlueRed Press Ltd. 2021
Designed by Elly Forty-Robbins
Type set in Raleway

ISBN: 978-0-7643-6211-8
Printed in India

Published by Schiffer Publishing, Ltd.
4880 Lower Valley Road
Atglen, PA 19310
Phone: (610) 593-1777; Fax: (610) 593-2002
Email: Info@schifferbooks.com
Web: www.schifferbooks.com

For our complete selection of fine books on this and related
subjects, please visit our website at www.schifferbooks.com.
You may also write for a free catalog.

Schiffer Publishing's titles are available at special discounts
for bulk purchases for sales promotions or premiums.
Special editions, including personalized covers, corporate
imprints, and excerpts, can be created in large quantities
for special needs. For more information, contact the publisher.

We are always looking for people to write books on new
and related subjects. If you have an idea for a book, please
contact us at proposals@schifferbooks.com.

CONTENTS

Project Difficulty Rating

 beginner   medium   🪶🪶🪶 more complex

INTRODUCTION

So what is millinery? A centuries-old craft. An art form. A melting pot of sculpture, fashion, textiles, theater, frivolity and formality, detail, and drama. A way to invite or deflect attention, to disguise or accentuate. An accessory that follows its own aesthetic, one that can finish an outfit yet surpass fashion trends and inspire and complement all ages, shapes, and sizes.

Traditionally created for women and often decorative, delicate, and intricate, couture millinery is carefully handmade to look effortless and almost "untouched." It comes in many forms—tall hats, small hats, perchers, pillboxes, headpieces, hair bands, and many others in between.

This book is designed to introduce you to this versatile craft and its wonderful materials and traditional methods, alongside evolved techniques and design advice.

Millinery encompasses a vast array of making techniques that differ from purpose to purpose, milliner to milliner; the composition of a brimmed winter hat, for example, will be quite different from that of a delicate headpiece. This book combines a selection of those techniques that I hope will be most useful and adaptable. Many have been acquired and developed from generous milliners in some of London's finest workrooms and educational colleges, while others have evolved within my own practice.

I have aimed to provide a comprehensive base knowledge, accessible for varied skill levels and budgets. Each project is marked with a skill rating to help you decide which is best for your current level.

The blocking projects are designed to guide you through working with each core material individually, in order to focus on and understand their unique properties, the way they feel and respond to the processes.

Discover how to make sculptural couture hats from flat patterns without the need for blocks, and to learn additional ways to trim your work. We will also consider how to produce millinery while being mindful of the impact on the environment, and some of the options available when it comes to this.

The projects are completed using hand sewing in order to show traditional couture methods and make them accessible to everyone. I have, however, given reference throughout the book of when a sewing machine could be used if desired.

Once you are familiar with the techniques and materials, you will be able to mix and match them with those from other projects; for example, a blocked brim could be teamed with a flat patterned crown and veiling. Inspiration for alternative designs also feature throughout.

The "Expanding Your New Skills" chapter aims to encourage the exploration of your own ideas and tastes, equipping you with the tools to create beautiful designs and work through any creative stumbling blocks.

If you are new to millinery, there is a list of useful millinery terms in chapter 1, and at the end of the book there is a guide to troubleshooting, the pattern library, and a suppliers list.

When it comes to materials and equipment, investing in high-quality products is recommended for high-quality results. However, high-quality results don't have to mean a huge outlay.

Hat blocks can be costly, and it can take time to build a collection. It's often considered necessary to have a wide range of blocks to create your hat designs, but this may not be realistic, especially when starting out. This doesn't have to be a barrier to learning, since many designs can be achieved by knowing how to adapt what you have. We explore how to make the most of a simple and widely available wooden block, where you could use alternative items such as wooden bowls, and how to create couture pieces without a block at all. Learn how to use this limitation as a positive challenge rather than restriction, through exploring the versatility of your materials and equipment, and push the boundaries with creative thinking. I hope you enjoy the activities in the book and have fun with your own creations!

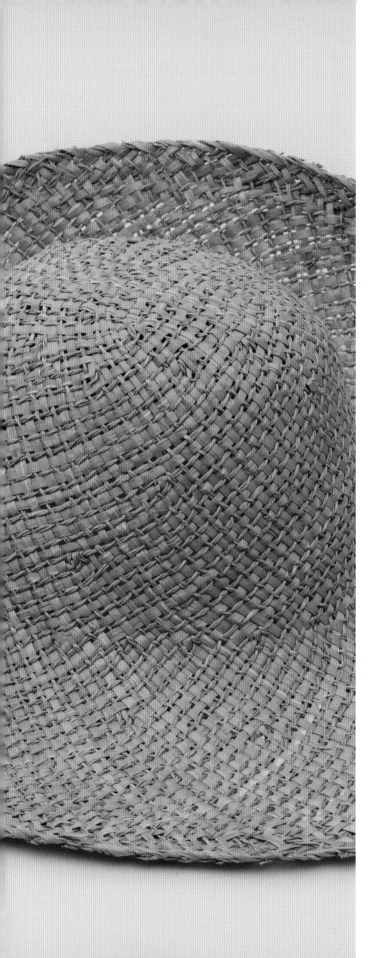

THE BASICS
WHAT YOU NEED TO KNOW BEFORE YOU START

Before you begin making hats, you'll need to familiarize yourself with the essential tools, materials, and stitches required. This chapter covers the essentials, desirables, and some additional options.

TOOLS AND MATERIALS

ESSENTIAL EQUIPMENT

These essential items will be needed for every project.

Thimbles (1a)
They come in different sizes, so it's best to try a few to find the perfect fit. Wear on your middle or index finger to help push the needle through material. Metal ones are best since they are most resistant to pressure.

Scissors (2 x 1b)
A sharp pair exclusively for fine fabrics. Another pair for buckram/paper, straws, and stiff materials. A pair of snips / small, sharp scissors for intricate work and cutting close to thread ends.

Needles (1c)
Straw needles, or "modistes"; nos. 7, 8, or 9 are best for fine hand sewing yet are strong enough to get through thick layers of felt and straw.

Pins (2 x 1d)
Strong steel "household" pins or 1" (2.5 cm) adamantine pins for blocking. Fine dressmaking pins for pinning fabrics. (There's more info on pinning in the blocking section, chapter 2.)

Tape measure (1e)
Essential for measurements.

Threads (2 x 1f)
Stock up on a range of colors, because the better the match to your material, the better the result. I find 100 percent polyester "sew all" threads are the best for all-around use.

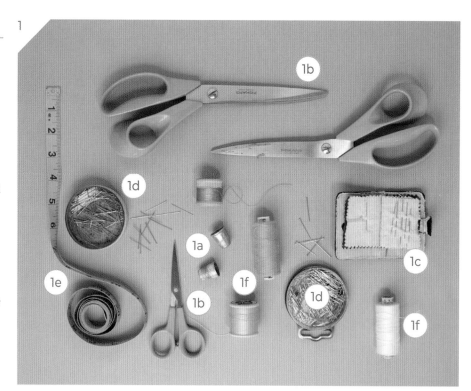

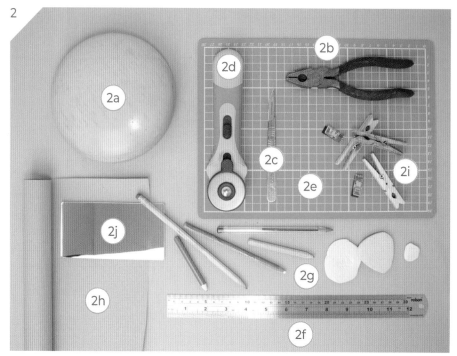

A percher or button block (2a)
Blocks are the wooden shapes that hats are traditionally formed on. The single block used in this book has a 6⅓" (16 cm) diameter, which can be used in many different ways.

Flat-nose and cutting pliers (2b)
Useful for removing pins from blocks and essential for cutting and bending wires.

Scalpel (2c), *rotary cutter* (2d), *and cutting mat* (2e)
For neatly cutting intricate lines and shapes in a multitude of materials.

Ruler (2f)
Metal or plastic, at least 11⅞" (30 cm) long. Metal is best for cutting with a scalpel.

Chalks, pens, and pencils (2g)
For marking measurements and transferring patterns.

Pattern paper / parcel paper (2h)
A roll of strong paper will be needed for transferring patterns.

Clothespins / bulldog clips / wonder clips (2i)
For holding wires in place prior to attachment.

Mirror (2j)
To check the positioning of your hats and trims.

3

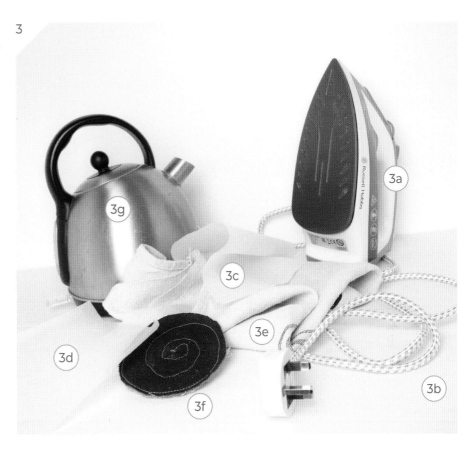

Iron (3a)
A steam iron is useful; however, steam can be applied with a damp cloth if required. Small irons are easier to handle but not essential. Be careful when using heat or steam.

Ironing board/surface (3b)
Flat, heatproof, clean surface for preparing materials.

Ironing/pressing cloths or press pad, offcuts of organza/organdie (3c), and baking paper (3d) make ideal protective layers that can be used between the iron and hat to protect it from burns and dirt. Keep separate ones for fabrics, straws, buckram, and felts. A calico cloth or dish towel (3e) is good for

dampening felt. Press pads (3f) are small, ideally round, handheld padded shapes, useful for protecting your hands and to give a soft surface under a material that can't be ironed on a flat surface.

Steamer/kettle (3g)
This doesn't need to be a professional hat steamer. A stove-top kettle, handheld steamer, or wallpaper steamer with the end cut off works equally well. Be very careful not to put your hands directly in the steam when holding your work over it, since it can quickly cause serious burns. Stand to the side of the steam and place the hat in it only with your hands below the steam.

Adhesives (4a)

It's a good idea to have a range of craft glues, fabric glues, and superglues on hand for occasional use.

Design tools

Notebooks/sketchbooks/paper (4b), pencils (4c), pens (4d), and paints (4e) for jotting down your ideas.

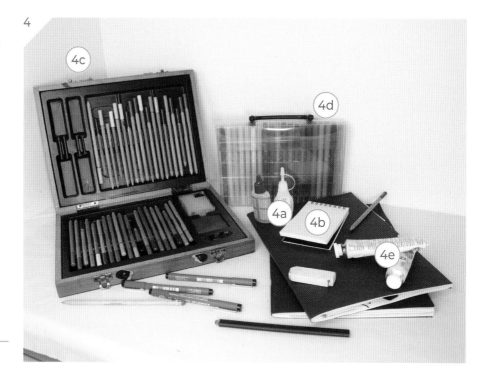

DESIRABLE EQUIPMENT

A range of different blocks

You may want to invest in additional blocks. A dome crown (1a) or simple crown (2 x 1b) and simple brim (1c) are versatile for beginners, but household items such as wooden cheese boards (1d) and fruit bowls (1e) can also be experimented with. (1f) shows a handmade buckram block, (3 x 1g) shows a range of perching shapes.

Hatstands (1h)

Useful for resting crown blocks while blocking on them.

Hat stretchers or expanders (1i)

Useful for stretching the head size of a hat, stretchers can be expensive but expanders less so.

Nylon/metal blocking spring (1j) / thick elastic (1k) / string (not shown)

Useful for blocking crowns; they pull down over the material, which helps the process.

Water spray bottle (2a)
For dampening felts, sinamay, or straws for blocking.

Metal suede brush
(2b) / toothbrushes / nail brushes
Brushes are great for neatening the direction of felt fibers.

Poupee / mannequin head / dolly head (2c)
Very useful for positioning hats while you work on them. They can also be used as blocks. A basic polystyrene mannequin head can be picked up for very little cost.

Curling tongs / wand (2d) and cardboard tubes (2e)
Great for shaping feathers, quills, and other trims.

Apron (2f)
For protecting your clothes from pins, rough materials, dye, fluff, etc.

Iron cleaner (2g)
It is vital your irons are kept clean, but inevitable they will get dirty, so this can come in very useful.

Masking tape / sticky tapes (2h)
Useful for temporarily securing items, removing fluff, etc.

Hairspray (2i)
Helps remove dried-on chemical stiffener residue and is good for lightly stiffening veiling.

Corset bone (2j) / palette knife (2k)
A strong, thin, flat, long, and flexible tool can help ease materials from blocks.

Bradawl (2l)
Useful for making holes in material or scoring lines in materials for flower making.

Small hammer (2m)
If your blocks are very hard or you find it difficult to push pins in, try gently hammering them.

Flat-tipped marker pens (2n)
A range of colors are great for coloring elastics and refining details.

Fabric dyes (not shown)
Although not covered in this book, dyeing materials are very useful when you require a specific color. They can also be used to dye feathers.

2

STIFFENERS

Stiffeners are required to give structure and strength to felts and straws and can be used on some fabrics when making flowers. There is a range of different types available from millinery suppliers; they are usually either chemical, alcohol based, or water based, with differing levels of toxicity and environmental impact, but the options differ depending on which country you are in, as does the method in which you use them. They all take practice in order to find the best method of application on your chosen material and its color. For example, some will leave a gray or yellowish tinge to white materials. Here are some general tips, but ask the supplier for tailored advice when purchasing.

Chemical stiffeners (1a)

They are very effective stiffeners, but most can be harmful to the environment and your health, so use in a well-ventilated area and take note of the warnings on the bottle. Sometimes these stiffeners can leave residue marks, but some can be dissolved by applying millinery thinners, hairspray, or even additional stiffener.

Water-based stiffeners (1b)

The water-based stiffeners are usually a synthetic polymer PVA solution, which is nontoxic; however, it can be toxic if burned. There are some available that are biodegradable. They can be diluted to your requirements.

Shellac (not shown)

This is a resin from the female lac bug. It comes ready to use or in flakes that need to be mixed with a solvent.

Starches (not shown)

Powdered starches are commonly made from rice, potato, or corn flour and need to be mixed with water. They can be shaped with heat once dry.

Gelatins (not shown)

These give an interesting light stiffness but can easily lose rigidity, especially in heat or humidity.

Stiffener brushes

I find that household paintbrushes around 1–1½" (2.5–4 cm) wide (1c) are best for stiffening. Keep different brushes for chemical and water-based stiffeners, and separate ones for straw, felt, and dark and light colors. It's usually best to apply sparingly and build up layers.

Chemical stiffener brushes cannot come into contact with water, so remove excess stiffener and wrap them tightly in metal foil, plastic wrap, or a sealed bag after use. (1d) If they are stiff when you next use them, stand them in stiffener for a few moments to soften. Brushes from water-based stiffeners can be washed in warm water.

Jars with lids

It's a good idea to keep separate stiffeners in labeled jars for different colors and materials (2 x 1e), to avoid contaminating them with unwanted colors and fibers.

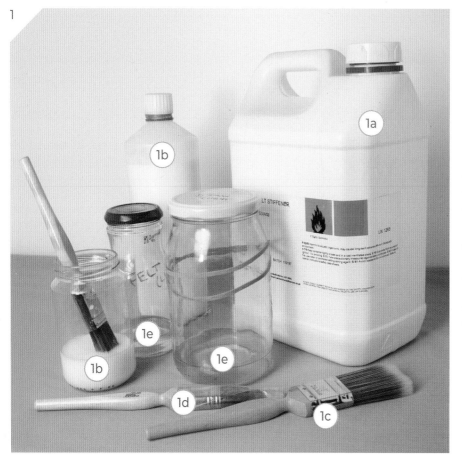

1

MILLINERY MATERIALS

CORE MILLINERY MATERIALS

The following four millinery materials are the most commonly used to form the base and trims for couture hats. They can be dyed, stiffened, and formed into 3-D shapes with water or steam and will keep their shape once dry.

Millinery felt

Felt is formed into two basic sizes:

cones/hoods (**1a**)—dome shaped, suitable for headpieces, and sometimes enough for small-brimmed hats.

capelines/flares (**1b**)—they have a rounded crown with a flat, brim-like outer. Suitable for medium-to-large-brimmed hats.

Craft felts or synthetic felts are not suitable for the processes involved in millinery; instead there are two main types of felt used to make cones and capelines, which are the following:

wool felt—100 percent sheep's wool. It is the cheapest of the millinery felts. It's stiffer, courser, and slightly harder to block than fur but can hold its shape better with less stiffener than fur.

fur felt—100 percent rabbit fur byproduct. Fur felts come in a range of different finishes and price ranges. Some examples are: regular, suede, and velour / peach bloom (these have fine fur fibers that are brushed smooth, giving different finishes) (**1c**), and melusine and salome (these feature longer fur fibers, giving an opulent look) (**1d**).

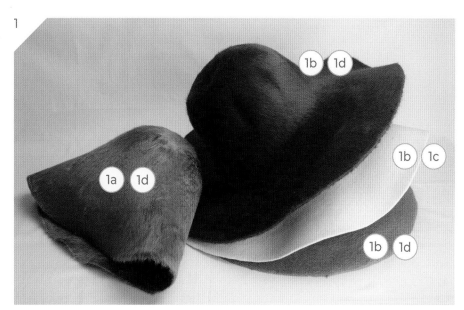

Sinamay

A strong, flat-woven material with a straw-like texture available by the yard/meter. It is created in the Philippines using fibers from the stalks of the abaca plant, a species of banana palm native to the area. It is available in a range of weaves, finishes, and qualities. Some examples are regular (**2a**), window pane (a crisscross pattern), tangle tuft (randomly textured), and pinok pok. (**2b**)

Buckram

Buckram is a thick canvas of varying weights and stiffness available by the yard/meter. Made from 100 percent starched cotton, buckram is a foundation material that gives strength and shape to the inside of a hat under fabric (**2c**). It is the modern replacement for sparte, a finer product now hard to source.

Straw

Straw comes in cones or capelines, like felt. A large range of weaves are available in differing qualities and price ranges; most are hand woven, while some are sewn from braid. They can be made from many plant fibers, such as boa straw, wheat straw, abaca, raffia (3a), seagrass (3b), or hemp, and commonly are made from the sisal plant. Cheaper versions are available in paper (3c). Some examples are parasisal (widely available, a smooth, fine weave made from sisal) (3d); sisal (also made from the sisal plant, with an alternative finish using a different weave); panama (available in many weave qualities, primarily made in Ecuador from panama straw, from the locally named toquilla plant); and parabuntal (the finest quality, of lightweight straw, highly desirable but less commonly available).

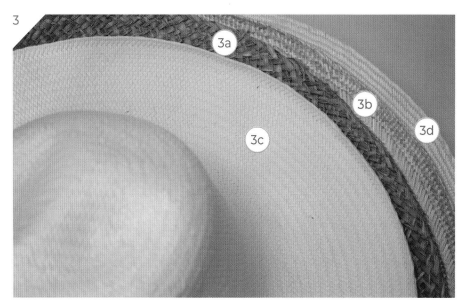

Other foundation materials and interlinings

Blocking net (4a)
Wide-woven, lightweight, stiffened cotton. A lighter, less strong alternative to buckram that can also be decorative.

Tarlatan (4b)
A very fine-woven, stiffened cotton, used to give a smooth finish over buckram or in thin bias strips to cover wired edges.

Fusible interfacing/webbing (4c)
An adhesive available in sheets, used to bond layers of material together with heat.

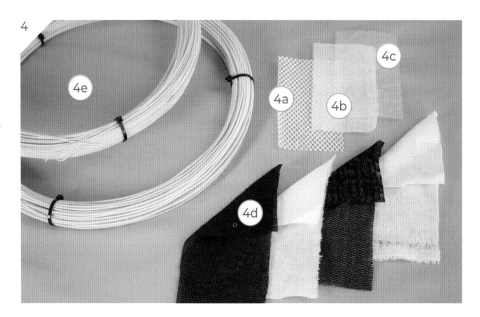

Domette and Staflex (4d)
Soft, fine-woven fabrics, sometimes with an adhesive backing, used to give a smooth finish over buckram or to add body to a material.

Millinery wire (4e)
This is a cotton-bound, sprung steel or copper wire available in different thickness, from stiff and strong through to very fine. In this book we will be using a strong wire with a thickness of 1.2 mm / 16 gauge; this will be used in the main construction of the hats. A finer wire with a thickness of 0.4 mm / approx. 46 gauge, will be used for trims and flower stems. (Find out more about wire in the wire exercise, p. 28).

TRIMMINGS

Tulle (5a)

A netting, usually with a stretch. Available by the yard/meter in synthetic or natural fibers, both coarse or fine.

Veiling (5b)

A stiff, synthetic, wide-weave netting.

Straw braid (5c)

Available in many weaves, widths, qualities, and materials such as polyester, paper, raffia, and plastic.

Crin/horsehair (5d)

A synthetic netting woven into a range of widths, from thin ribbon and tubes to fabric on the roll, known as flat crin or couture crin.

Millinery petersham ribbon (6a)

Millinery petersham is a stiff, ridged ribbon made from cotton, rayon/ viscose, or a blend. It has a scalloped edge, which allows it to be shrunk and curved with hot water / steam. Sometimes called grosgrain, but this is a term for a wider range of ribbons, most of which have a straight edge and aren't flexible. Always check the edge when buying. It can be used as a trim as well as inside the headline of a hat.

Feathers and quills (6b & 6c)

There are many types of feather that can be used in millinery. They can be curled, cut, and dyed to suit your designs.

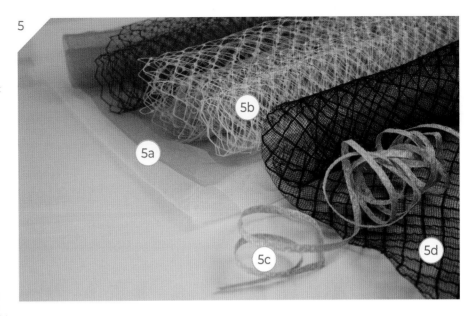

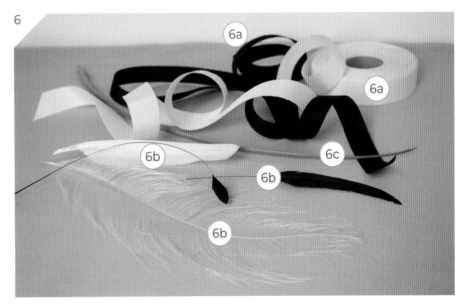

Woven and Nonwoven materials

Fur / faux fur (not shown)
Available in many thicknesses and qualities. Can be used to cover hats or made into trims.

Leather
Soft, fine leathers such as lamb nappa (**7a**) are best since they can be effectively blocked by dampening and stretching. Available in a range of finishes, such as patent (**2x 7b**) or suede (**7c**).

Thermoplastics
A range of heat-moldable plastics that can be used as an alternative foundation material to buckram.

Plastics
Some plastics are recycled/recyclable and can be very versatile, such as polypropylene, PETG, and acrylic sheets, which are available in many finishes and thicknesses and can be heat-molded. (**2 x 7d**) Other plastics such as PVC are usable but arguably less environmentally friendly. (**2 x 7e**)

Woven materials
Natural fabrics can be blocked effectively over a foundation material by pulling the fullness out of the weave. Materials such as silks (**3 x 8a**), wools, natural velvets, and linens work well. Sheer materials such as organza (**8b**) are great for trims. Synthetics such as polyester and nylon do not hold their shape as well when blocked, but can also look effective if used in trims.

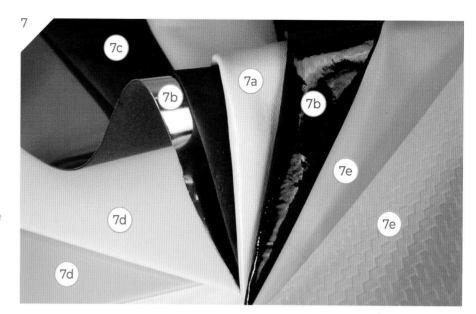

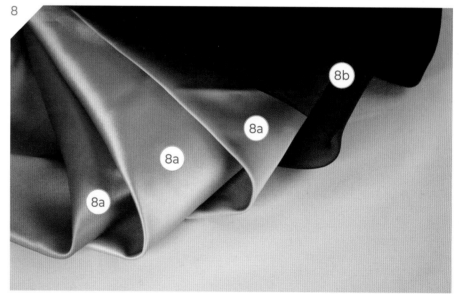

THE BIAS EXPLAINED

The term "bias" is used for the grain line that runs diagonally through woven fabric at a 45-degree angle to the straight threads of the weave (the warp and weft). Cutting patterns on this line gives fabric more stretch.

1. If you pull a piece of woven fabric from top to bottom (on the straight grain) or side to side (on the cross grain) along the straight of the threads, it won't stretch. If you pull it diagonally (on the bias grain), it will stretch since the threads can move together and apart where required, meaning it can be manipulated around curves without creasing. This is vital in millinery, since curves form the basis of all hats and brim edges. If fabrics are not cut and worked on the bias, the fabric won't drape or fit around the shape.

2. To find the true bias, fold over a corner of the fabric (forming a triangle) so that the up/down and left/right threads align exactly. The diagonal line the fold creates is the bias line.

3. You can extend the line to reach the measurement you need by pulling the corner of the fabric farther into the center.

4. The bias line can be marked by pressing with an iron or your fingers.

5. Fabrics will need to be cut using the bias regularly in millinery. Many of the patterns in this book are marked with arrows. These indicate the straight/cross grain line. If the arrow is placed along the direction of the threads, the pattern will thus be positioned for correct use of the bias.

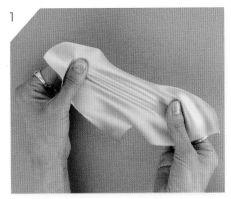

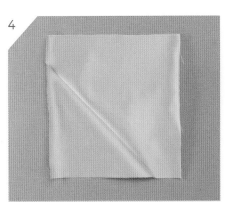

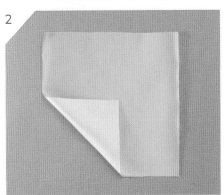

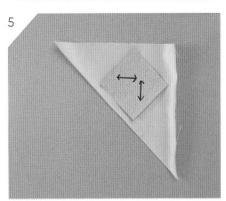

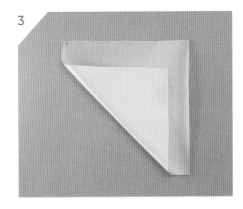

THE ANATOMY OF A HAT

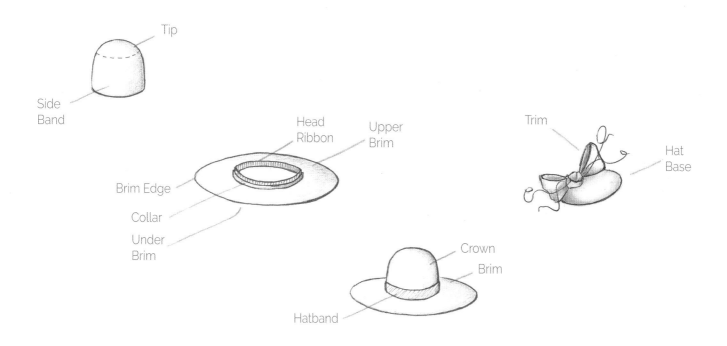

TAKING A HEAD MEASUREMENT

To fit a hat to the head, whether it's an Alice band or full hat, you'll need to work with the measurements of the head in order to fit it correctly. The average female head size is around 22½" (57 cm); males, roughly ⅘" (2 cm) larger.

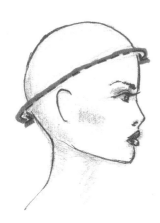
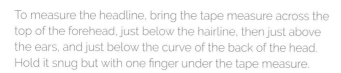

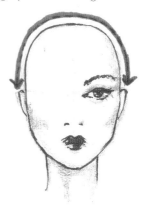

To measure the headline, bring the tape measure across the top of the forehead, just below the hairline, then just above the ears, and just below the curve of the back of the head. Hold it snug but with one finger under the tape measure.

To measure the depth of the head, measure across the top of the head from just above each ear.

USEFUL MILLINERY TERMS

Alice band
A wired headband that sits across the head. Hat bases and trims attach to this.

bias
The term used for the grain line that runs diagonally through woven fabric, at a 45-degree angle to the straight threads of the weave (the warp and weft). Cutting patterns on this line gives fabric more stretch. See p. 19 for more info.

binding / bound edge
The name and method given to a material that will cover and finish a raw edge.

blocking
The process of molding and fixing a millinery material to a hat block through the use of heat, steam, and pins to form the base of a hat.

blocks
Solid forms in the shape of a hat or headpiece that can be blocked (see above). Usually made from wood but can be handmade from other materials.

CB/CF
Reference to the center back or center front of a hat.

cocktail hat / percher hat
A small blocked hat, usually finished with a petersham ribbon inside, like the blocked hats in this book.

collar
The part of the hat that stands upright at the headline.

couture millinery
Headwear, often decorative, that is handmade using the finest materials and involves very little or no machine work. It is hand crafted and hand sewn where possible from start to finish with no factory-made components.

display head
A decorative mannequin used to display finished hats.

fascinator/hatinator
Terms sometimes used for headpieces, with fascinator being a smaller version and hatinator a larger version.

frond
The fine parts of a feather that grow from the spine.

hatter
Makers of what are traditionally thought of as men's hats, such as trilbies, fedoras, bowlers, and caps, although there is crossover with millinery.

head fitting
The way in which the hat fits at the headline, or on the head.

headline
The center part of the hat that meets the head.

headpiece
A term used widely for smaller brimless hats, particularly those with small bases made up mostly of trimmings, or trims on Alice bands.

head ribbon
The ribbon (usually petersham but sometimes leather) that sits inside the hat at the headline or inside a base.

milliner/millinery
The term traditionally used for the creation of women's hats. It originated in the early 1500s, when it was coined from reference to hatmakers from Milan (Milaners), which was a hub for the making, selling, and buying of fashionable products at this time.

N–S, E–W (north–south, east–west)
Reference to working around a shape in opposite positions to ensure even distribution of material.

petersham / petersham ribbon
A stiff, ridged ribbon with scalloped edges that can be curved or shrunk with hot water or steam. Made from cotton, rayon/viscose, or a blend.

poupée / dolly head / mannequin head
A dummy head usually made from stuffed canvas or wood, which can assist in the making of hats. Cheap versions are available made from polystyrene.

quill/spine
The center part of a feather, which can be stripped and shaped for decoration.

ready-to-wear hats
Hats made from a combination of hand sewing and machine- or factory-produced components .

SA / seam allowance
The extra material given to a fabric pattern in order to sew the seam.

toile/mockup
A prototype of a hat, something produced to develop an idea or test it before the real item is created.

top fabric
The fabric that will be seen on the finished hat.

wrong side / right side
Wrong side is the underside of a piece of fabric, the side that will not be seen.

MILLINERY STITCHES

MATERIALS
- thread
- swatches of fabric

EQUIPMENT
- sewing kit

Throughout this book, I have used contrasting thread so stitches can be seen clearly. When you are making the projects, choose a thread that matches your fabric as closely as possible. I recommend practicing these stitches on a piece of fabric before trying them on a hat. They require a lightness of touch to give the impression the pieces of your hat have just drifted into place. Overhandling and tight stitches will spoil the effect.

Always wear a thimble when sewing. It takes practice to use but will protect your finger, which will otherwise get very sore with repeated pushing of the needle through materials. If your thimble slips around, try sticking a piece of masking tape around the inside of it to give some grip.

Knotting your thread to begin a stitch
Before hand-sewing any stitch, the thread first needs to be knotted so it sits in the material securely and won't slip out as you stitch.

1. To create a knot, wrap the thread around your index finger three times, keeping hold of the short end with your thumb, and the long end in the other hand. Roll the threads back and forth between your index finger and thumb so they twist up. Roll the thread off the end of your finger and pull it tight to create a knot. Sew over the knot twice before beginning to stitch.

Tying off thread to finish
2. I use this method most commonly; sew over the last stitch a couple of times with tiny stitches. Pass the needle under the threads, then through the loop this creates to form a knot. Pull tight. Repeat the knot two or three times to make sure it won't come undone.

1
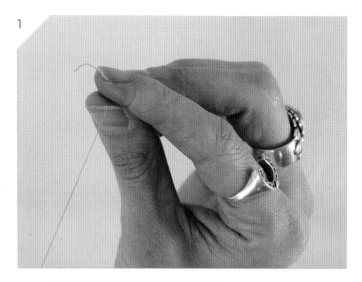

2
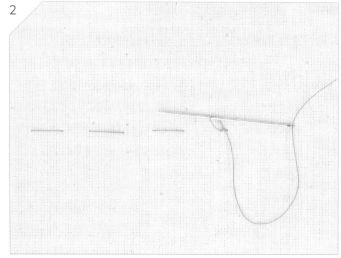

Millinery wire stitch

Also known as buttonhole stitch or blanket stitch, it's used to sew wire onto or just above the edge of the base material.

3. Oversew a couple of times over the edge of the shape and around the wire to secure, then take the needle under these stitches.

Move the needle about $^2/_5$" (1 cm) along the edge, then bring the needle up through the material from the underside, about 3 mm into the material edge. A loop will form; bring the needle up through the loop from the underside and pull closed, creating a knot. Aim for the knot to sit on the edge, since this will keep the wire secured. Take care not to tangle the thread.

Repeat the steps until the end, then oversew and knot the thread to finish.

Wire stitch in a fold

Similar to the wire stitch. Sometimes it is necessary to sew wire into a dip, curve, or fold of material. This is how the wire is sewn into the round bases in the blocked hats in this book.

4. Pin the wire into position by sliding pins from the outside, over the wire and back out. Looking into the fold, push the needle down on one side of the wire to the outside of the material and back up as close as possible, catching a few fabric fibers and making a tiny dot stitch on the outside; the needle needs to be brought up on the other side of the wire. Repeat in the same place to create a loop over the wire. As you pull the thread back up, take the needle through the loop it creates, then pull it tight so it sits over the wire. Move along $^2/_5$" (1 cm) and repeat the stitch; however, this time it needs to be made only once.

If working in a fold of felt, try to go through only the top portion of felt fibers rather than down and out to the other side; this will be quicker and stitches won't show on the other side.

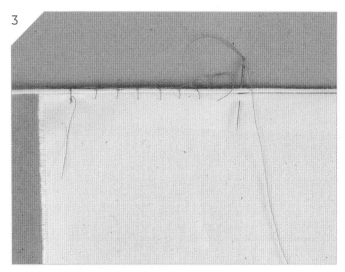

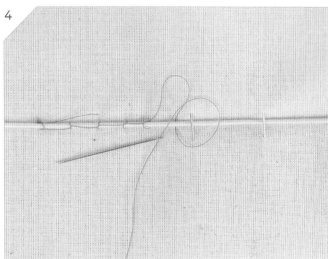

Backstitch

Used to attach crowns to brims and in seams, and to join layers of material, including brim edge binding.

5. Bring the thread up through the material and along $\frac{3}{5}$" (1.5 cm). Push the needle down to the underside and take it back halfway along the stitch (0.75 mm) before bringing it back up through the fabric. Bring it along another $\frac{3}{5}$" (1.5 cm). The new thread should be overlapping the previous thread by half. Repeat; the needle should come up next to where the thread has gone back down into the material on the previous stitch. Always keep the overlapped threads on the top, since they create a smooth, secure foundation.

Slip stitch

Used in folds, joins, and hems where stitching needs to be invisible.

6. Starting from the underside, slip the needle into the fold, then bring it out to the surface. Take it directly into the other side of material. Take the needle along the underside of the material $\frac{1}{5}$" (0.5 cm), then back up and directly back into the fold on the other side. Take the needle along another $\frac{1}{5}$" (0.5 cm) within the fold, then bring it back out and into the other side of material as before. Repeat the steps until the end and tie off, hiding the knot under a fold or inside. Gently pull the thread to create a smooth join, but not so tight it puckers the fabric. The stitches should be hidden when pulled. Within time you should be able to make these stages in one movement. If using on a hem, make the stitch on the flat side of fabric as tiny as possible, instead of $\frac{1}{5}$" (0.5 cm).

Stab stitch

Another invisible stitch, used to attach felt items or petersham binds, or to attach some trims.

7. Bring the needle from the underside or the inside of the bind and up to the surface, then take it back down as close to the first stitch as possible, so it catches just a few material fibers.

If the stitch is to be seen on both sides, repeat the stabbing motion on both sides, angling the needle as it goes through from top to bottom. If it is to be seen only on the top (for example, for a trim), the stitches can be longer on the inside. When sewing petersham, stitch just inside the curves on the edge, catching every third curve.

5
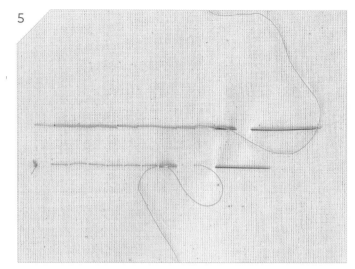

6
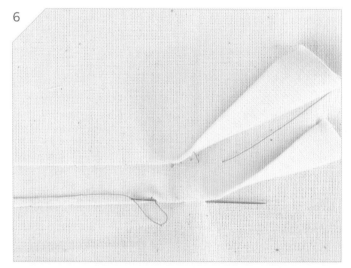

7
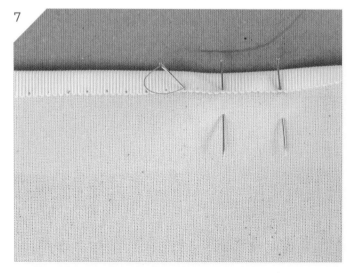

Tie tack

A tiny, singular stitch used to hold in place delicate items such as veiling, bows, and drapes.

8. Bring the needle up from the underside, keeping a long loose end of thread on the underside. Push the needle back down through the material, very close to where you came up, creating a tiny stitch. Tie the loose ends of the threads with a double knot, then snip off the thread close to the knot.

Running stitch

Used to gather material in linings or veiling.

9. The length will vary depending on the thickness of material and size of gather required. Oversew with a backstitch a few times at the beginning of the stitches, to avoid the thread pulling out. Sew from topside to underside along the fabric in a straight line, at even intervals. On completion of the stitches, pull gently on the thread at the end to gather the material, and secure in place by oversewing with a few backstitches and knotting. Sometimes the gather will need to be pulled from both ends, in which case undo the oversewn first stitch.

Tacking stitch

Used to temporarily hold materials in place.

10. This is created in the same way as the running stitch, but stitches are generally larger (make them roughly $\frac{2}{5}$"–$\frac{3}{5}$" (1–1.5 cm) and don't need to be gathered. They are removed once the item is properly secured.

8
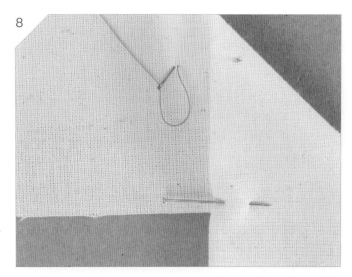

9
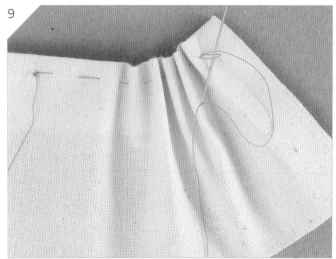

10

Diagonal stitch

A very useful stitch, used to sew in linings and to join overlapping seams, among other things.

11. It's like the running stitch, but the top thread is sewn at a diagonal instead of straight. The thread on the underside will appear in parallel straight lines.

Rolled-edge stitch

Used to secure rolled edges.

12. Begin with the knot under the roll. Bring the needle up through the roll, angled toward the inside of the hat. Push the needle back down into the base of the material, under the roll and angled toward the outer edge of the hat—this should tuck around the roll and help draw it in. With the needle on the outside of the roll, bring it back up very close to where it came out, and up into the roll again, angling it toward the inside of the hat as before. Push it back down into the base of the material and repeat.

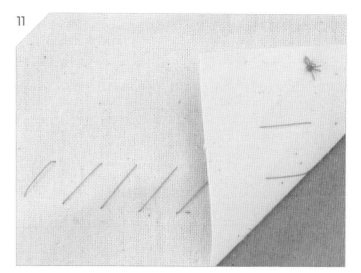

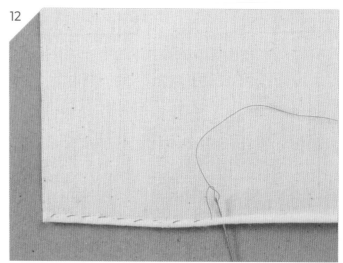

Felt stab stitch

Used to join decorative edges of felt invisibly.

13. Lay the felt edges together with the right sides of the main surfaces facing up. Slide the needle into the center of an edge, and back out 1–2 mm into the main surface. Take the needle back down in the same spot it came out, but angle it diagonally. Pass it through the center of the edge again, then into the center of the adjoining edge and out 1–2 mm into the main surface. Repeat this until the end. It should create a zigzag of thread concealed inside the felt.

Felt whipstitch

Used to neatly and securely join pieces of felt or fur without the need for folded seam allowances.

14. Hold the thin cut edges of the felt parallel, with the right sides of the main surfaces facing inward. Starting at the top, sink the needle slightly into the edge on one side, then, at a slight angle, pass it directly through to the other edge and out. Keep the stitches very small, close together, and within the cut edge; try not to puncture the main surfaces on both the right and wrong sides. This will ensure the stitches are barely visible when pulled tight. Bring the thread back across to the first side to repeat the process, working in a looping motion.

15. Once finished, lay the felt flat, then pull the threads tight by gently hooking them from the top down with your needle—this helps bury them in the felt. Brushing over the surface will help create an invisible join.

> **Tips**
> • If you cannot avoid seeing a contrasting thread on your hat—for example, sewing a white trim on to a black base—sew using the lighter color, then color in the thread with a pen to match the darker color.

13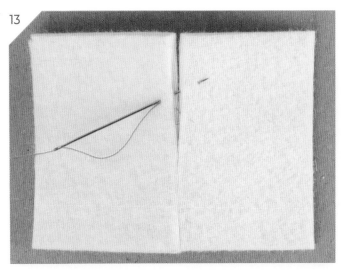

14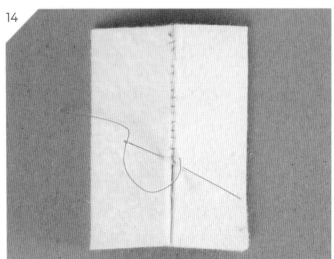

15

GETTING TO GRIPS WITH MILLINERY WIRE

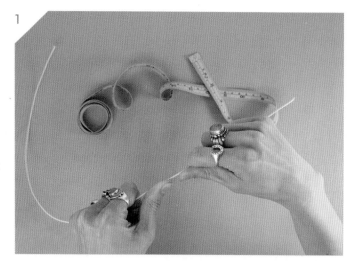

MATERIALS
· wire
· thread

EQUIPMENT
· wire cutters / pliers
· pencil or pen

This warm-up exercise will help you get to grips with millinery wire. Learning how to prepare wire structures well is important to the success of the entire hat. A badly fitting wire that has been pulled together unnaturally can start to work free over time and distort your work. Wires are the bones of the hat and need to be properly shaped in order to produce a high-quality, long-lasting, and comfortable piece from the inside out.

Instruction can take you only so far, but with practice your hands will become familiar with the process, and it will become second nature to create accurate structures. Here we will make a wire oval to fit your own head, which can be used as a quick guide for checking the head size of hats by placing it at the headline. The more accurate you can be with it, the more useful you will find it.

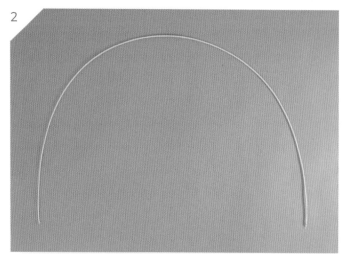

1. Take your head measurement, add 2" (5 cm) to the length, and cut this total from the wire (in this instance I have used a 22" (56 cm) head measurement, so a total of 24" (61 cm). For an accurate and easy measurement, hold the tape measure along the outer curve and shuffle your fingers along the curve, holding the tape bit by bit as you measure.

The spring needs to be removed from the wire. Hold the wire steady in one hand, and hold between your thumb and fingers in the other hand, with your thumb against the outer curve. Apply an even pressure with your thumb and run it slowly along the curve so that it begins to straighten it. Pressure needs to be firm yet not too heavy, so that the curve starts to flatten but kinks aren't introduced. Don't move too fast, since it's easy to burn your thumb from friction.

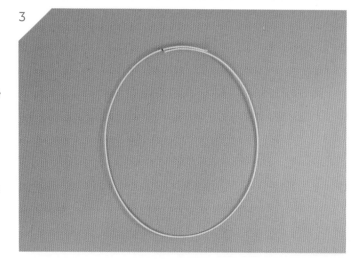

2. The wire now needs to be made completely flat. Lay the wire on a table, then trace along the wire with your eye to see where unwanted curves are by seeing the gaps between the wire and the table. Then gently glide your fingers and thumb against the curves as before, until they are flat. The wire doesn't have to be completely straight along the length; some curve can remain. Repeat the process until the entire wire sits flat to the table.

3. Keeping the wire on the table, gently bend it into an oval that fits your head comfortably. Mark 2" (5 cm) along from one end—the other end should overlap and sit perfectly with this mark.

Binding the wire join

4. Cut a piece of thread approx. 39.5" (1 m). Double it over and fold the loop around the middle of the overlap. Bring the loose ends through the loop and pull tight.

5. Firmly wrap the thread around the middle of the wire a few times. The loop will slip if bound in one direction but stay firm in the other. Now start binding the thread around the wire, working toward one end and spacing each wrap roughly 2 mm apart. Once you reach the end, wrap four or five times over to secure, then start wrapping the thread back toward the middle and to the other end. **(5a)** Once you reach the other end, wrap four or five times over, then bring it back the other way to the middle.

At the middle point, twist the threads on themselves, then wrap the ends of thread in opposite directions around the wire a couple of times, so they cross over each other, before knotting them tightly to secure **(5b)**. Try the wire on your head to check that the fit is correct. You can adjust the shape slightly if needed.

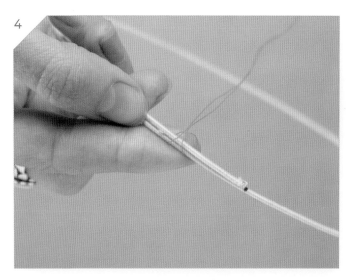

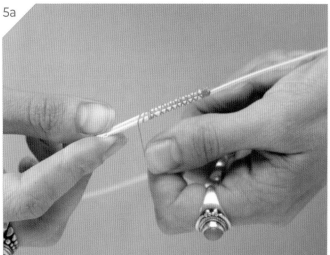

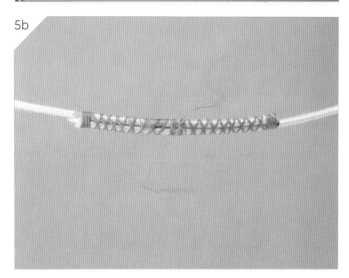

PETERSHAM HEAD RIBBONS

The most common way to finish the inside of a couture hat or headpiece is with a millinery petersham ribbon. Its purpose is to cover any joins between a crown and brim, or raw edges of a hat base, and to cover the area where the lining is attached. It is also there to protect the hat from dirt during wear.

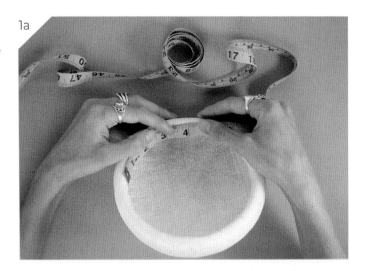

Petersham comes in many widths; the size used for a hat that fits the whole head is usually number 5, while smaller hats and headpieces work well with number 3.

FITTING AND SEWING A PETERSHAM TO THE HEADLINE OF A FULL HAT OR A HAT BASE

MATERIALS
· hat base
· petersham ribbon (enough to fit the headline plus 1⅕" [3 cm])

EQUIPMENT
· dressmaker's pins
· scissors
· thimble
· thread
· needle

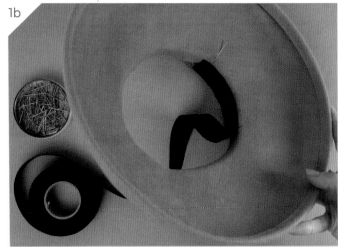

Positioning the petersham

1. Measure the circumference of the hat's head fitting **(1a)**, then add 1⅕" (3 cm) to the measurement. This is the amount of petersham you will need. You can cut it or pin it in straight from the roll.

Position and pin the end of the petersham ⅗" (1.5 cm) over the center back (CB) line; position it so it sits slightly lower than the edge of the base (cocktail/percher hats) or headline **(1b)** (full hats) (this is so it won't be seen when the hat is worn).

2. Pin the petersham around the shape, with the sharp end of the pins facing down into the crown to minimize scratches to your hands when sewing it in. Be careful not to let the ribbon slip up or down but let it remain an even height.

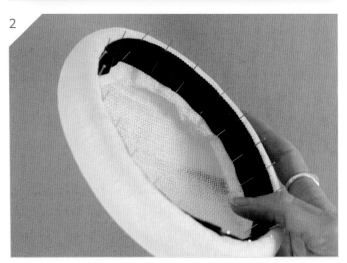

3. Once you reach the back, fold the end over at the CB line and pin in place.

Sewing the petersham

4. Thread the needle and knot the end of the thread. Bring the needle under the petersham and push it up through the base and through the edge of the ribbon at the CB. Now push the needle down slightly into the surface of the hat, close to the edge of the petersham, where your thread comes out.

5. Angle the needle so it follows the edge of the ribbon, then bring it back up through the ribbon again. Try to make the stitch length two petersham "ridges" long. Keep repeating this around the whole shape and keep the stitches tiny and even, since they will be seen (see images).

Once you reach the CB, bring the needle to the underside of the petersham and secure the thread by oversewing and knotting on the folded ends.

Tips

. You may be surprised at how often millinery creations get worn back to front. This can be avoided by adding a little decorative stitch to the center front of the petersham, which acts as a guide on how to wear it.

. A hat that is too big can be made slightly smaller by easing the fullness into a smaller-sized head ribbon, and one that is too small can be stretched by steaming and pulling over a block of the right size, if you have one.

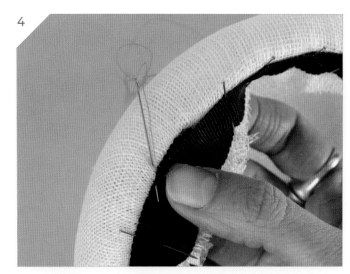

4

5a

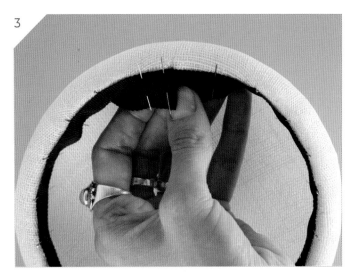

3

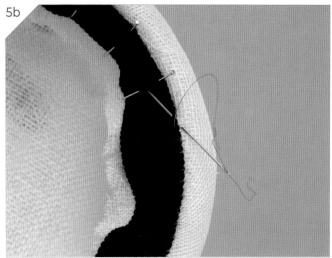

5b

BLOCKING

BLOCKING AND TRIMMING CORE MILLINERY MATERIALS

A wide variety of hat designs doesn't always call for an equal quantity of blocks, which may be welcome news when you are new to millinery and unsure about what to invest in. Working with a limited selection can often be a positive, since such restrictions can encourage inventiveness.

Every project in this chapter has been produced using a simple, round button hat block (also known as a percher or cocktail hat block), since this is one of the most affordable, accessible, and versatile shapes available. The one used here is 6⅓" (16 cm) in diameter, but other sizes are available.

You could use any small block shape; however, you may require some additional skill and artistic license in blocking, attaching, and fitting the trims.

In this chapter we explore the properties of the four core millinery materials (felt, sinamay, straw, and buckram), learning ways of blocking and trimming each material exclusively. Many of the techniques can also be adapted to other materials.

General Blocking Instruction and Advice

Preparation

Blocks always need covering prior to use. This protects them from wear and tear and protects the hat from any dirt or residue that may be on the block. Blocks can be covered in a clear polythene bag taped on the underside, in a layer of plastic food wrap, or in a smoothed-down layer of metal baking foil. **(image 1)** Foil is probably the most economical, being plastic-free and longer lasting (it can be wiped clean). It is also far more heatproof so doesn't stick to your materials if overheated through ironing, which can be problematic with sinamay and straw. Use a little sticky tape on the underside if it slips around. However, it's better to use plastic wrap if you can't completely smooth out the ridges in foil, since they may show through on your material.

Wearing an apron will protect your clothes from pins, stiffener, and water.

Always measure around the largest part of your block and add a couple of inches before cutting the blocking material.

Steaming/wetting

Blocking can be achieved by using either steam, a water spray, or wet cloth and iron; the best technique depends on the project.

A hat steamer is not necessary for steaming. A tabletop wall steamer (with its nozzle cut short) or a kettle work well. Hold the switch of the kettle down or keep the lid open so it can continue boiling while you work. It can be very easy to burn yourself on the steam, so take extra care to keep your hands behind the nozzle and well away from the steam.

Pinning

I recommend using strong household pins or adamantine pins. I use household pins since they are slightly shorter and stronger than regular dressmaking pins so can be pushed into blocks without bending too often. Occasionally, drawing pins / push pins are useful for pinning under blocks but are not recommended for general blocking, since they can't be positioned close enough together, leading to a lower-quality finish. Household pins take more practice to use initially, but you will get better results.

Always wear a thimble on the finger that pushes in the pins, or your fingers will soon get very sore.

Hold the pins either between your index finger and thumb, pushing the pinhead with your middle finger, or between your middle finger and thumb, pushing with your index finger. If you're struggling to secure the pins, a small hammer or pin pusher can help, but it's best to practice doing it yourself. (image 2)

When pushing pins into the wood, angle their flat tips toward the edge of the fabric so the fabric is well anchored and doesn't slide off them when you pull in the opposite direction. (image 3)

Always work pins into the block, alternating them in opposite sections (north–south [N–S], east–west [E–W], etc.) so the fabric is evenly dispersed. Pins should eventually sit around $\frac{1}{5}$" (0.5 cm) to $\frac{4}{5}$" (2 cm) apart, dependent on the type of material, fullness, and amount of stretch required.

It tends to be easier to use your body as additional support for the block as you pin; however, this isn't always possible on large shapes. Always work on a surface at a height that doesn't strain your back.

On woven materials, always guide the bulk of material toward the bias points. Placing the bias at CF, CB, and sides gives the most pleasing finish. Fullness can be removed only along these "stretchy" areas. Trying to remove fullness from the straight woven areas will only tire the material, and it may fray.

2
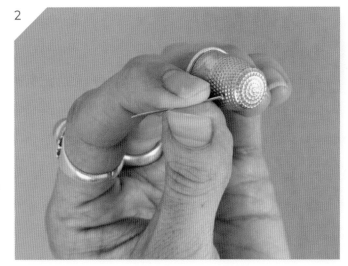

3
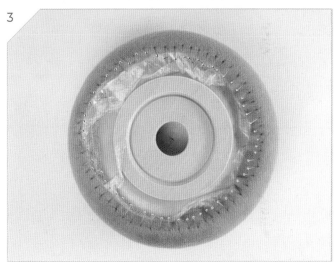

Reposition pins when necessary to ensure an even dispersal of material and avoid wrinkles.

Removing the block

A small pair of flat-nose pliers can help remove pins from the block. (image 4)

When removing the material from the block, trim back the excess raw edges, then loosen the material from the wood with your hands in an even, gentle motion. Wiggle your fingers between the layers, grip the block, and ease off the material. If it's still hard to remove, gently slide a corset bone or palette knife under to help ease it off. (image 5)

Making a wire for your blocked base

Cut a length of millinery wire the circumference of the underside of your block, plus 2" (5 cm) for overlap. Shape the wire so it fits perfectly to the block with the exact overlap. Bind the wire join with thread. (image 6) (see p. 28 for further wire instruction). Slot the wire into the blocked base and pin inside. (image 7)

Sew using the wire stitch in a fold. (image 8)

Blocking on a full crown block

If you were to prefer an alternative to the button used in these projects, I would recommend a dome crown block in your own head size or the average of 22½" (57 cm). This type of block, although more expensive, is particularly useful since it can be adapted into different crown shapes through creative cutting and hand shaping, and the flat underside can also be used as the top of the block. This will give a different look to the base.

To block over a full crown, your chosen material needs to be pulled down smoothly over the sides of the block, an inch or so lower than the height required for your finished piece. A blocking spring, wide elastic, or string can be fastened around the sides of the crown to help keep the material in place alongside pinning. (image 9) The blocking guidance related to specific materials in these projects can also be applied to full crowns.

7

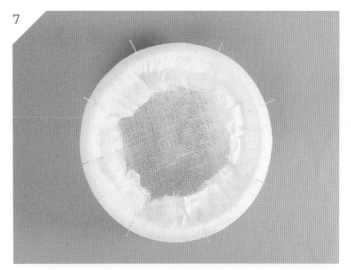

8

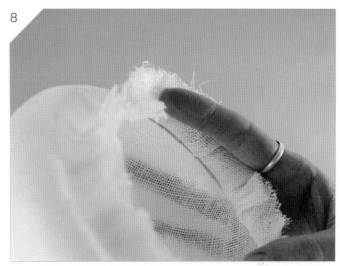

9

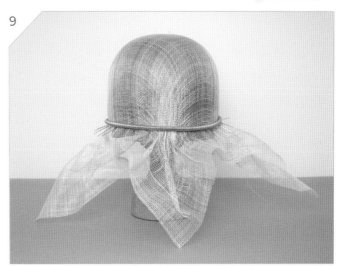

Sinamay with Sculptural Ruffle and Spirals

MATERIALS

- 29½" (75 cm) white sinamay
- 29½" (75 cm) black sinamay
- 11⅞"(30 cm) silver sinamay
- NB: The better the quality of sinamay, the easier it will be to use and the better the finish
- medium or strong millinery wire (enough to fit inside the headline of the base with 2" (5 cm) overlap)
- matching thread
- no. 3 petersham to fit the headline
- elastic (see p. 126)
- lining fabric (see p. 130)

EQUIPMENT

- sewing kit
- button block
- pressing cloth (organza or organdie)
- scalpel and cutting mat (optional)
- steam iron or dry iron and water spray
- tailor's chalk
- wire cutters / pliers
- ruler
- steamer/kettle
- stiffener

An eye-catching headpiece, fun but formal for weddings and events

1. Cover your block with plastic wrap or foil. Cut three squares of white sinamay on the straight of grain. Make them large enough to cover your block, plus a couple of extra inches (5 cm).

1

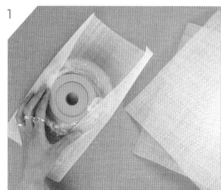

2. Lightly steam the sinamay or dampen with a water spray. You can redampen it at any point if it becomes too dry and stiff.

3. Bring two layers of the sinamay together, aligning the weave of each piece. Using a thimble, begin pinning the sinamay to the block. Start with the straight edges first (where the weave of the threads is straight across and down). Make sure the sinamay is positioned evenly over the block, so you have enough material around all edges to pull on without it fraying. Smooth the material snug around the block, and pin through into the underside of the block, angling your pins in toward the center.

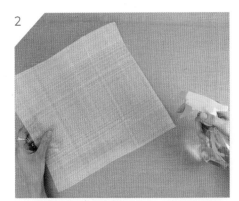

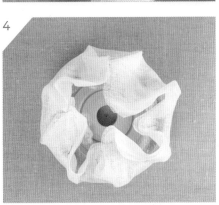

4. Now stretch the sinamay at the bias points, by pulling the corners with one hand and holding the block in the other. You might find it easier to steady the block against your body. Pin into these areas.

Between each pin, smooth the sinamay firmly over the block with your fingers to remove any wrinkles and puckers, then pin. Work around the shape in opposites (N–S, E–W, etc.) to ensure an even dispersal of fullness. Try to keep the fibers in the weave straight on the top surface by pulling along the woven lines, since this will look far better than a wobbly weave!

5. You can leave the blocking at two layers; however, adding a third with its bias points placed in the direction of the previous layers' straight points gives a more dense-looking coverage and, in my opinion, a higher-quality finish.

To add the third layer, begin pinning in the same way as before, but remove each pin from the underlayer and replace in the top as you work around. The true bias points will sit at the center front (CF), center back (CB), and sides of the finished shape.

Some sinamay comes prestiffened; if yours is not, it will now need stiffening. If you're not sure, stiffen anyway. If using water-based stiffener, apply while the shape is wet; if using chemical stiffener, wait until it's dry, then apply. After stiffening, leave to dry.

6. Press the shape under a pressing cloth to give a smooth finish. Keep the iron moving so as not to scorch the sinamay, and pay particular attention to ironing smooth any curves, and the gathers toward the pins.

Trim back any excess sinamay, leaving around 1" (2.5 cm). Remove the pins, then iron over the area where the pins were. Remove the sinamay from the block.

Shape and insert a wire into the base (see p. 37), fit and sew in a petersham ribbon (see p. 30), then fit an elastic (see p. 126).

Making the ruffle

7. Using tailor's chalk and a ruler, measure and cut a bias piece of black sinamay 19⅔" (50 cm) along the top. Measuring at a right angle from the center of this top edge, mark down to create the width at 11⅞" (30 cm). Mark this distance in a couple of locations either side of the first mark. Now draw the bottom edge along these marks. The diagonal ends (which are on the straight of grain) should measure around 16½" (42 cm).

8. Bring together the diagonal ends, matching top edge with top edge. It will form an awkward shape initially but, once pinned, will form a tube with a diagonal seam. The corner tips should poke over the join by ⅖" (1 cm).

9. Sew with a seam allowance of ⅖" (1 cm), using a small backstitch, or straight stitch on a sewing machine. Remove the pins as you go.

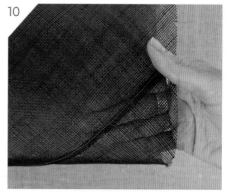

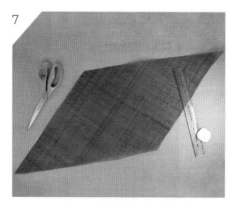

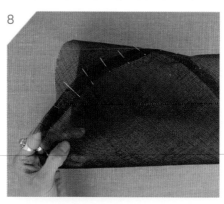

10. Iron the seams over in the same direction. This is easiest to do by placing one hand inside the tube, covering your hand with a press pad or folded cloth to protect it from the iron, then iron on the outside. Trim back the seam to 5 mm.

11. Spray the sinamay with water to soften it, so it is easy to manipulate and doesn't split. Fold the loop in half by bringing one edge over and toward the other, concealing the seams inside the fold. Make sure the unfinished edges meet along the bottom, then iron the top folded edge. Your seam should create a "V" shape.

12. Working on approx. 4" (10 cm) sections at a time, use a steam iron or iron and water spray to press the folded edge. Stretch and hold the heated area for a few seconds until it cools.

13. Repeat until the whole folded edge has been stretched to capacity.

14

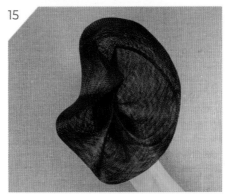
15

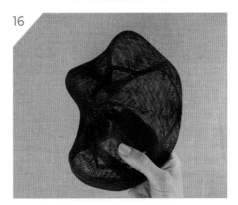
16

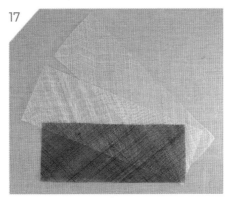
17

14. Dampen the sinamay again. Gather and pinch the bottom raw edge into five or six points in one hand.

15. Now start playing with the folded edge to form waves in the other. For this arrangement I created a large curve near the top, with a few smaller ones over to one side; however, this is open to your interpretation, so don't worry if yours doesn't look exact. Try the shape either on the hat base, your head, or a mannequin so you can understand how it will look when worn.

16. Once you are happy with the shape, pin the gathers in place, sew them together with a few stab stitches, and trim off any scruffy fibers.

Bias-cut sinamay spirals

17. Cut three pieces of sinamay on the bias, one black at 4" x 10" (10 x 25 cm) for the back of the hat, and two silver at 4" x 11⅞" (10 x 30 cm) for the front.

18. Fold each piece in half, lengthways, finger-pressing as you go, then dry-iron them to achieve a crisp edge.

19. Using a ruler and scalpel or scissors, trim down the side of the raw edges to take off any uneven or rough fibers.

20. Open the fold, then fold in and press the raw edges toward the center crease, leaving around a 2 mm gap in the middle. This avoids bulky rough edges poking through to the outside. Fold back in half and iron again.

21. Cut the ends of the strips at an angle, following the straight of grain. The point should be at the fold.

22. Fully open out one side of the fold. Cut away ⅖" (1 cm) from the top edge of the outermost fold, stopping about 5 mm before the fold line (see image). Fold the piece back over, then do the same on the other side and fold this back in.

23. With the piece unfolded at the center, trim off the center point to create a straight line; the straight line should sit a few millimeters above the points of the outer folds.

24. Wet your finger and fold in the raw edges in the center of the straight cut.

25. Fold the two longer ends over the raw cut ends (see image), then fold the whole strip back in half and iron, making sure all sides meet neatly.

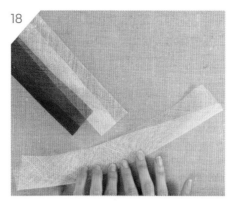

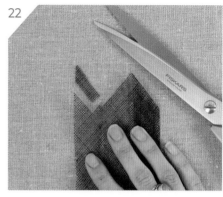

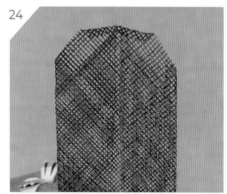

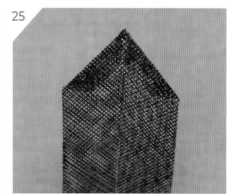

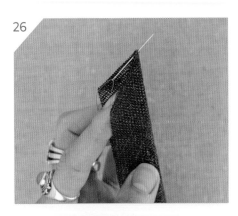

26. To sew, knot your thread and bring the needle up through the fold to the point (see image). Slip-stitch down to the corner, then reverse and slip-stitch back over a few stitches to secure. If your sinamay has a more open weave and the tip is fraying, poke the ends in with a pin, then add a tiny amount of stiffener, and iron to seal.

Repeat the process for the ends of all strips.

Curling the spirals

27. Curl the strips by wafting lightly through the steam, keeping your hands well away from the steam. Then hold each one around a cardboard tube for a minute or so until dry, which will set the shape. If you'd like a different-width spiral, try other household objects such as a broom handle or curling tongs (no steam required for this one). You can also control the size of spiral by simply setting it with your fingers. The black one here has been bent at a right angle in the middle, then curled by hand.

Add elastic to the base now for ease (see p. 126), placing the bias at CF (see pp. 19 and 21).

Attaching the trim

28. Position and pin the ripple to the base, then stitch down, using stab stitches, going through the base. The stitches can be longer on the underside of the base, but keep them small on the top.

Position the silver twists inside the ripple by pushing them between a fold. Check that you like it by trying it on a head, then pin to hold in place and sew with a few stab stitches. Try to hide the stitches; however, their position depends on where you have placed the spirals. I have tie-tacked the spirals to the edge of the ruffle to help control their shape (see image).

29. Last, arrange the remaining twist over the raw edges at the back of the ripple, pin, then stab-stitch through this into the base a few times to secure.

I tweaked the ends of the spirals with curling tongs to give more definition.

Why not try . . .
• adding lots of spirals of different lengths and widths, or multiple ruffles in smaller sizes.

Straw with Hand-Shaped Drape and Rolled Edges

MATERIALS

- parasisal straw hood/cone
- medium or strong millinery wire (enough to fit into the base with 2" [5 cm] overlap)
- approx. 6½ ft. (2 m) of fine millinery wire. This hat can be made without wiring the edge; however, a large trim such as this won't hold its shape so well without.
- 9" x 9" (23 x 23 cm) veiling
- no. 3 petersham to fit the headline
- matching thread
- elastic (see p. 126)
- lining fabric (see p. 130)

EQUIPMENT

- sewing kit
- button block
- pressing cloth (organdie or organza)
- iron
- wire cutters / pliers
- water spray or kettle
- stiffener

A statement piece, designed to turn heads

Blocking the straw base

1.   Cover your block with plastic wrap or metal foil. Dampen the straw hood with a water spray or lightly steam so that it is evenly damp but not soaking wet. Leave a couple of minutes to soften.

Position your straw hood over the block, making sure the center "X" of the weave sits centrally on the block.

1

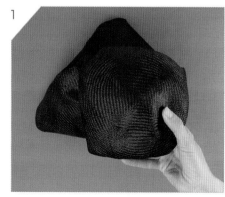

2. Begin molding the straw over and around the edge of the block with your fingers. You may find this easier to do by steadying it close to your body or the table, so it doesn't slip, and work on the opposite side. Smooth down one section of straw over the edge and to the underside of the block, then pin through the straw into the block with a couple of pins. Two are useful in the first instance to avoid slipping.

3. Work around the shape, molding the straw under and adding pins in opposite locations (N–S, E–W, etc.). Keep checking that the middle "X" of the straw hasn't moved from the center and is keeping an even shape. It is easiest to pin following the lines of the center "X" first, in order to keep them straight and keep the lines of the weave from looking wobbly. Also keep an eye on how the weave looks around the edges, to make sure they remain straight.

4. Pin until their coverage is approx. ⅖" (1 cm) apart and the straw sits smoothly and evenly over the block without any puckers (see image).

Iron the shape under a pressing cloth. Glide the iron over the straw in circular motions, being careful not to scorch the surface. Take the tip of the iron right up to the pins. Ironing will flatten any rough or bumpy areas.

Stiffening the shape

5. If using water-based stiffener, you can apply even if the shape is damp. If using chemical stiffener, wait until it's dry, then apply. Stiffen around the edge and right up to the pins. Be sparing with the stiffener, since the shape doesn't need to be drenched.

After stiffening, leave to dry, then iron the surface of the straw through your pressing cloth as before; this gives a beautiful polished finish. Take your time to get it smooth and you will be able to feel the difference by running your hand over the surface.

Removing the straw from the block

6. Unpin the straw and carefully cut into the excess by snipping through the straw near the pin line.

7. Cut the whole piece away so you are left with a skirt of straw. This will be your material for free-form hand-shaping.

Remove the straw from the block, then shape, bind, and insert a wire into the base (see p. 37). The "X" of the straw should sit evenly at the CF and CB. Choose which side you would like to be the front, then place the wire join so it sits at the back.

Fit and sew in a petersham ribbon (see p. 30) and elastic (see p. 126).

8. Under the pressing cloth, press the straw loop to remove any creases and kinks with a steam iron or iron and damp cloth.

9. Cut through the loop at a sharp angle.

10. Trim off the edges to leave a smooth shape.

Wiring the edge

11. Measure around the edge of the straw, add 2" (5 cm) to the measurement, and cut a fine millinery wire to size. Fine wire can be easily straightened when it is sewn to the straw. Place the wire on the reverse of the straw (the side with small knots and loose ends). Position it roughly ⅖" (1 cm) in from the edge. Starting 2½" (6–7 cm) along from the end of the wire, sew the wire around the entire shape, using the wire in a fold stitch. Stop around 4" (10 cm) from the wire overlap. If required, trim any excess wire so the overlap is around 5 cm. Bind the join (see image), then continue sewing over it to finish.

6

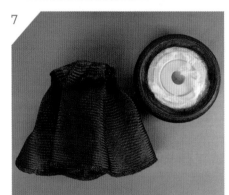

7

8

9

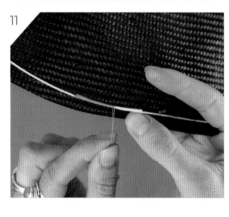

10

11

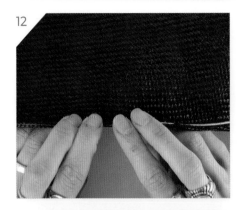

Hand-shaping the trim

This style is created as a guide, so don't worry if it doesn't look exactly the same. You will find your own hand-shaping style by letting the material lead you. Your work can be reshaped, so loosen up and see where it takes you! This technique requires a lightness of touch to avoid it looking forced, lumpy, or tired. Try to work with the weave of the straw; you will notice if it is being pulled unnaturally, so don't take it somewhere it doesn't want to go. If this happens, try guiding it in another direction to keep its smooth "bounciness." Make sure the straw doesn't become too wet, and let it dry for a few seconds after each new movement to let it set.

14. Lightly steam the straw to soften. Ease in a couple of soft folds along the length of the shape, then create a gentle bend halfway down. Work the folds in by smoothing your fingers along from the center out toward the tips, bending the wires to complement and secure the line this creates.

15. Roll the center point to create a swirl, then mold over the top of the right-hand piece.

16. Curl the tip of the right-hand piece around, and bend the left side over toward the right.

Rolling the straw edges

12. The corners can be fiddly and start to fray in the process, so paint with a little stiffener and leave to dry first. Work on a small section (roughly 2"–4" [5–10 cm]) at a time with this technique and move gradually along. To begin the rolling, first fold the very tip of the straw edge inward, between your fingers and thumbs. Then encourage the straw to roll over on itself by moving it back and forth until the roll becomes small and even, the raw edge is concealed, and the wire is encased in the roll.

13. Sew the rolled edge, using the rolled-edge stitch (see p. 26). Reroll each section just before you sew to get the neatest finish. Pull the thread snug but be careful it doesn't snap. Pay extra attention to corners and the areas where the weave sits with the fibers poking out. At the end, bury the knot under the roll.

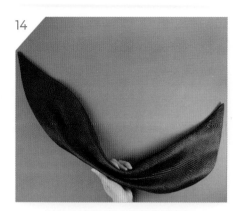

Compiling the hat

17. Put the base onto your own head or a mannequin and position the shape onto the base. When you are happy with how it looks, pin the shape to the base, then tie-tack, taking your thread through both layers a couple of times, and triple-knot the thread for strength. The pins in images a and b show where I have pinned and then sewn; the pin at the top of the trim shows where I have tacked the two sides together. Your locations may vary, since the exact shape of the trim and base will undoubtedly vary. The shape needs to be secure enough so it doesn't wobble, and stitches should be avoided directly at the front, where they will be most noticeable. Check that the shape looks smooth and doesn't pull unnaturally before sewing.

18. To give interest to the back of the hat, veiling has been added. Cut a square of veiling roughly 9" x 9" (23 x 23 cm), then snip off the thick edges.

19. Pinch the middle of the veiling between your fingers, slightly off-center, then gather the pinch to create an attractive drape. Sew the pinched area with a few stitches.

20. Arrange the veiling at the back of the hat, then sew to the base with a few stab stitches, securing on the underside of the base. The tips of the veiling can be snipped into to soften the edges if desired.

17a

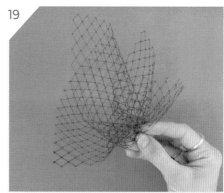

19

17b

20

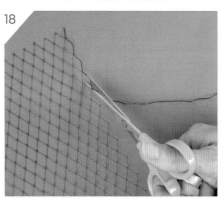

18

Tips

• To block a straw brim, secure the straw at the headline with string first, then pull the straw diagonally down toward the brim edge, following the line of the weave as you pin. Do so in both left and right diagonals to ensure a smooth and even finish.

• Free-form hand-shaping doesn't always need a wire in the rolled edges—try it without if your shapes are small. Just be sure to add plenty of stiffener afterward.

Why not try . . .

• creating new shapes by cutting into the shaped straw, to accentuate the silhouette.

• hand-shaping entire hoods or capelines straight onto an Alice band; no base required.

• swapping straw for felt, which can be hand-shaped very effectively with a little steam.

Buckram and Leather with Angular Fabric Bow

Playful pinks with fun feathers, great both for parties and formal events

MATERIALS

- soft, fine leather; I have used lamb nappa
- 3 buckram squares (see step 1)
- medium/strong millinery wire— enough to fit inside the base with 2" (5 cm) overlap
- for the bow: minimum 7⅞" x 15" (20 x 38 cm) fabric on the bias. I have used a crepe jersey, but silk, duchess satin, and medium-weight cottons work well depending on the look you require.
- 6⅓" x 13⅜" (16 x 34 cm) buckram on the bias
- 3" x 9" (8 x 23 cm) bias strip of satin
- matching threads
- 6 coq feathers
- no. 3 petersham to fit the headline
- elastic (see p. 126)
- lining fabric (see p. 130)

EQUIPMENT

- sewing kit
- button block
- iron
- wire cutters / pliers
- baking paper
- bowl of warm water
- cloth/dishcloth/sponge
- fabric glue

Blocking the buckram

1. Cover your block with food wrap or foil. Cut two layers of buckram, large enough to cover over your block and around the bottom, plus around 2" (5 cm) to pull on and pin into.

1

Working with one piece of buckram at a time, spray the buckram with water so it is thoroughly dampened and soft but not dripping (too much water will start to wash the stiffening starch from the material).

2. Pull the buckram over the block at the straight of grain, and pin these four points first.

3. Now begin pulling the fullness of the material from the bias points around to the underside, working in a N–S, E–W fashion. Keep pulling and pinning until the shape is completely smooth. Repeat with the second layer, replacing pins as you go.

Leave to dry, then dry-iron the surface to a smooth finish. Press firmly through a piece of baking paper to protect the iron from the adhesive and avoid scorch marks on the buckram. You can press directly but will need to clean your iron afterward. If your leather is very thin, you may need a layer of tarlatan to give a finer surface texture (see p. 16).

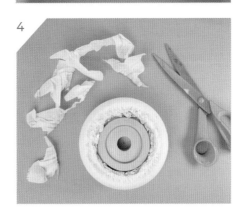

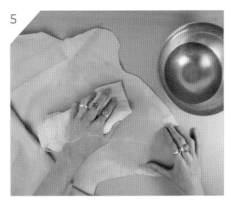

4. Remove the pins but leave the buckram on the block. Trim the raw edges on the underside to remove excess bulk

Blocking the leather

5. Choose a part of your leather that you want to feature on the block and lay wrong side (the textured side) up. Using a clean sponge or cloth, wet the leather evenly with warm water so it becomes soft and stretchy.

Due to its nature, leather will undoubtedly come with some imperfections, so choose the best section you can find while remaining as economical with the piece as you can. Always work with the smooth side of the leather up; the rough suede side is the underside.

6. Place the leather over the block and begin stretching and pinning it in N–S, E–W, as with the buckram layer (however, there is no bias). Pay particular attention to the curves and underside. Keep blocking until there are no wrinkles or puckers (see image).

The leather can now be smoothed over even more by ironing through the baking paper; this also helps the leather stick to the buckram underneath. Leave to dry, then cut away the remaining leather.

7. Unpin one-quarter of the shape. If the leather is stuck well to the buckram, go to the next step. If the leather lifts up, unpeel it to the rounded edge and add a line of glue. Make sure it is behind the line where you want your wire to sit (marked with the arrow here). Smooth back down the leather, replace a few pins to hold, and repeat around the whole shape (see image). Leave the glue to dry for a few minutes.

Unpin and remove the shape from the block. Due to the firmness of the buckram, you may need to loosen it all around the edge and use a butter/palette knife, or another pair of hands!

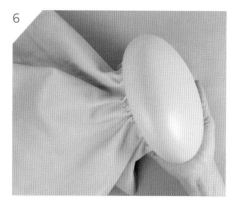

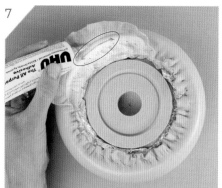

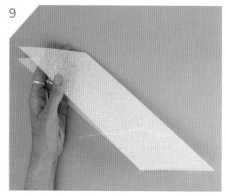

Fitting the wire and petersham
8. Shape, bind, and insert a wire to fit inside the underside of the block (see p. 37). Sew the wire to the buckram by lifting up the leather (see image). Once it's sewn, glue down the remainder of the leather edge.

Fit and sew in a petersham ribbon (see p. 30). The leather should be soft enough to sew through like any other fabric.

Making the fabric-covered bow
9. Take the 6⅓" x 13⅜" (16 x 34 cm) bias piece of buckram for the bow. Fold it lengthwise down the middle, then cut the ends at an angle, using the grain line as a guide. Cut both ends parallel to each other.

10

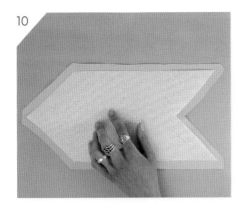

10. Open the buckram out, then lay the buckram strip on your top fabric (on the bias, wrong side facing up), and cut a piece roughly $^3/_5$" (1.5 cm) larger than the buckram. Draw around the buckram first if you find it easier.

11. Snip into the fabric at the inverted point, leaving roughly 2 mm uncut, and snip the points flat.

12. Fold over the fabric seam allowance and pin.

13. Tack down the fabric to the buckram with a tacking stitch.

14. Fold in half and pin the two sides together, snipping into the fabric at the points to remove bulk where necessary.

15. Slip-stitch the edges together; use the needle or a pin to push down any excess bulk at the corners inside. Add an extra stitch or two to the corners to neaten if required. If it's hard to tie off the thread, just run the slip stitch back along the length an inch or two to secure.

Remove the tacking threads, then iron the shape through a cloth to neaten the edges.

11

12

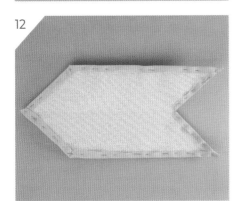

13

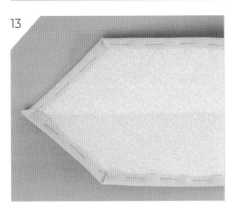

14

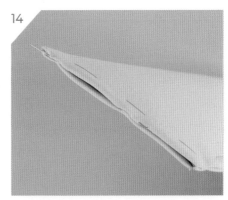

15

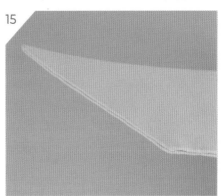

16. Lightly steam the shape again to gently soften it, so it can be neatly bent into the desired bow shape (see image). Then add a few stitches through the center to secure.

17. Cut the coq feathers into shape and bind them in two sets of three (see p. 110-113).

18. Stitch the bound areas through the center of the bow.

19. Take the bias strip of satin. Fold the long edges into the center and iron them.

20. Gather the end with your fingers, then sew this to the underside of the bow. Just catch the surface layer of fabric; there's no need to go through the buckram. The stitches don't need to be neat here.

21. Wind and drape the strip around the bow twice, then sew underneath again. Snip off the excess.

Position the bow onto the base and secure by stab-stitching through the base and bow multiple times in three hidden areas (see the pins in the image for locations).

The hat has been finished with a lining (see p. 126) and elastic (see p. 130).

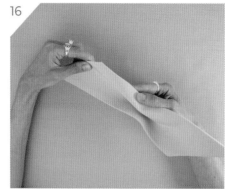

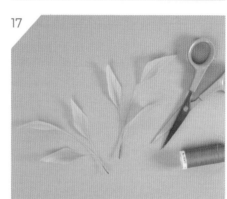

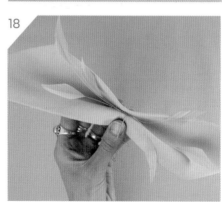

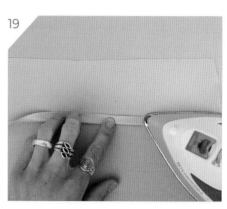

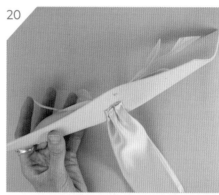

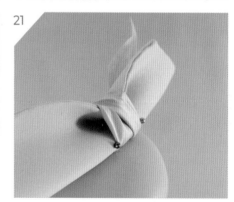

Why not try . . .
· mixing up different textures, patterns, and colors. Switching up the materials can make it suitable for any season.

Felt Percher Hat with a Brim

An elegant and dressy hat for the cooler months

MATERIALS

- felt capeline—I have used a peach bloom, but any felt is fine.
- felt offcuts if you would like the trim a different color; here I have used tonal shades.
- no. 3 petersham to fit the headline
- medium or strong millinery wire— enough to fit around the brim edge, plus 2" (5 cm) extra
- elastic (see p. 126)
- lining fabric (see p. 130)
- matching thread

EQUIPMENT

- sewing kit
- button block
- brim block / wooden bowl/plate or similar
- bowl of water or water spray
- iron
- pressing cloth (thick cloth or dishcloth)
- tailor's chalk
- pencil
- sandpaper
- masking tape
- wire cutters / pliers
- wire suede brush / firm toothbrush
- steamer/kettle
- stiffener

This book didn't seem complete without explaining how to construct a blocked hat with a crown and brim, so in this project we incorporate a brim block. I have, however, used a wooden bowl rather than a real brim block, to show how household items can be experimented with before investing in real blocks. If you choose to try an alternative to a real block, you may need to add something additional to secure your pins if the surface is hard to pin into, such as taping some layers of thick string around the underside.

Preparing the blocks

1. Cover your blocks with food wrap or foil. Stiffen the inside of the felt, using your chosen stiffener.

Mark on the size of your block's head fitting by placing the block onto the brim, protecting the brim with masking tape, then drawing around the crown block. Make sure it sits centrally by measuring up the sides of the brim. Your drawn line can then be used as a guide for blocking the headline. Your blocks will inevitably be different from these, but if you are using a small block for the crown like this one, try to use a brim block that is smooth across the top, without holes, "collars," or flat areas made to fit full-sized crowns, since it can be difficult to block over them well. This bowl has a raised circle in the middle, but it is smaller than the crown, so it won't cause a problem.

We will block the brim first. This is recommended if you are using a single capeline or cone; if you end up short on material, the crown can be stretched over the block easier, or a full crown shape can be extended with a strip of matching material and covered with a side band. The brim cannot be extended in this way; if it is blocked after the crown, the remaining brim section may end up with a large hole in the center (head fitting), which is more difficult to "shrink."

Blocking the brim

2. Place the capeline over the steam for five to ten minutes until it becomes soft and malleable (keeping the felt moving, and hands low and away from the heat). It is more efficient to place it inside a plastic bag and tie the bag loosely around the bottom, turning it occasionally for ten minutes or so, since the steam will penetrate the felt better (see image). Alternatively, you can immerse it in warm water for thirty minutes or so until the

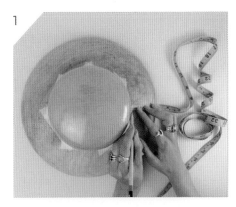

water sinks into the felt. Gently wring out the excess.

3. Remove from the steam and pull over the brim, pinning the outer edge at four opposite points around the underside of the shape.

4. You can soften the felt more once it's been slightly secured. To save lifting the heavy block to the steam, dip a cloth in a bowl of water or use a water spray, and work the steam into the felt with the iron for a few seconds, one section at a time. This also tends to be more precise.

5. Reposition pins if required as the felt stretches. Keep pinning until the brim is smooth and secure with pins.

6. Now block the felt up into the headline by working the steam in with the wet cloth and iron, pulling up one small section at a time and working in opposites as usual. You won't be able to see your drawn headline at this point, so keep placing the crown block at the center to get an idea of where to block to. Block about 1" (2.5 cm) inside the head fitting. You may need to work around the shape a couple of times to pull all the fullness out of the felt, to create a smooth headline. Stretch it as much as possible so there is the maximum felt available to block the crown.

Leave to dry overnight.

7. Once it's dry, remove the pins and redraw the crown in the center with tailor's chalk; this will be your guide for cutting.

Blocking the crown

8. Cut ⅗" (1.5 cm) inside the drawn line to separate the crown felt from the brim.

9. Resteam the remaining felt for a few moments, then place over the crown.

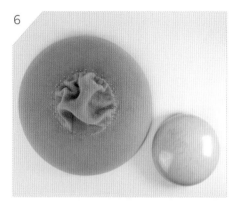

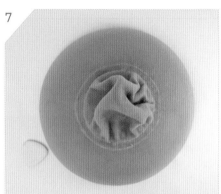

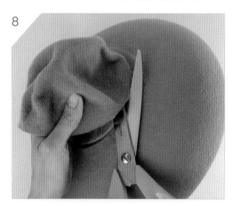

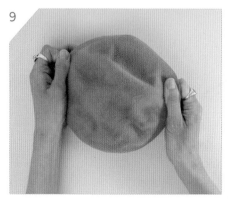

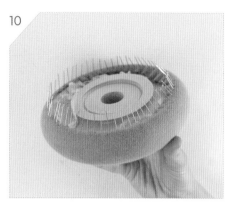

10. Block and pin as before until it is smooth. You may find you need to stretch the felt a lot to fit over the crown block, in which case using the wet-cloth-and-iron method tends to be more effective. You can use pliers to grip and pull the felt if you wish. Because the felt is limited, you may not be able to block it all the way around the underside of the block with excess to pull on, but as long as it reaches the bottom edge it will be sufficient. Once complete, leave to dry.

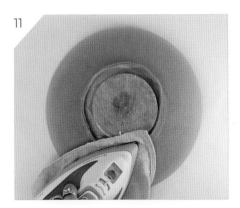

Creating a collar at the headline of the brim

11. Returning to the brim, take the damp cloth and use the tip of the iron to press against part of the felt at the head fitting, then lift and hold it for a few seconds until it cools and sets. Repeat around the headline to create a collar. The collar will sit inside the crown and should be positioned just inside the guide that was drawn onto the block at the beginning (see image). Leave to dry.

12. Sew a tack at the CF and CB (this "block" is the same all around, so I chose this myself).

13. You can take the brim line to the bottom of the block, as I have done here, or choose a shorter brim width. If you want it shorter, measure an equal distance up from the bottom of the block, all the way around, and draw a chalk line. Just bear in mind you will need at least $\frac{4}{5}$" (2 cm) extra below this line for turning under and enclosing the wire. You will need to draw this line onto the block too, in order to shape the brim wire.

Remove the pins, and trim off the excess from the edge, leaving $\frac{4}{5}$" (2 cm) extra for the turning (see image). If the shape feels soft in some areas, apply a little more stiffener to these parts now.

14. The UK chemical stiffener that I used sometimes leaves residue, which can be dissolved with hairspray.

Shape and bind a millinery wire to fit your chosen brim edge (see pg 28).

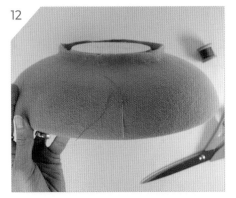

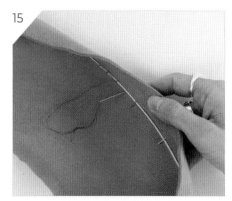
15

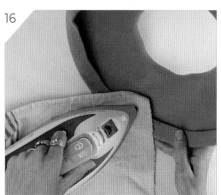
16

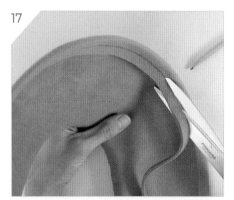
17

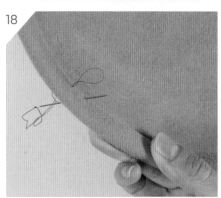
18

Finishing the brim edge

15. Pin the wire to the underside of your brim and sew, using a wire stitch.

16. Using a damp cloth, iron the edge of the felt over the wire, remove the heat, and hold a few seconds until cool. Be careful not to pull on the shape, since this will distort it, and don't overwet it, since this will also distort the shape.

17. Mark ⅖" (1 cm) along the folded edge (use a pencil here since it's more precise and will be cut off), then carefully trim back the fold to this line. Keep the scissors at the same angle all the time, and take your time to get an even cut.

18. Sew the fold, using a stab stitch. Pull the stitch securely, but not so tight it creates dents in the felt.

19. Press through a slightly damp cloth again to finish. You can soften this edge with sandpaper if you wish.

Pin and sew in a petersham to the head fitting (see p. 30).

Joining crown and brim

20. Now, working with the felt still on the crown, remove the pins and draw a pencil line around the bottom of the block, making sure it is even all around.

Sew a tack at CF and CB, remove the felt

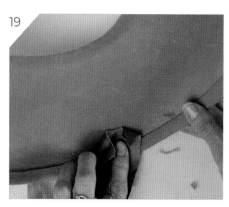
19

20

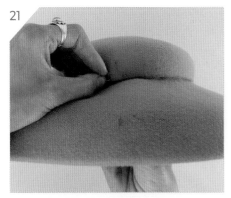

from the block, and cut at the pencil line.

21. Place the crown on top of the brim, positioning the CB and CF together. Pin the CF and CB first, then sides, then in between if required. Fold the petersham back underneath and grip it with your other hand in order to access the inside and to get a firm hold.

22. Sew the crown to brim, using a long backstitch.

Making the hatband

23. Take the piece of felt that was cut from the outer brim edge. If it's circular, cut it so it is one long length. Working in 7⅞" (20 cm) sections, iron with a damp cloth for roughly ten seconds to work in the steam, then stretch it and hold until the steam has dispersed and it's cooled. If you let go too soon, it will shrink back (see image). You need a straight length long enough to extend around the headline, and deep enough to cover the majority of the height of the crown. I recommend measuring this out with a ruler and pencil, then cutting with a scalpel or rotary cutter alongside the ruler.

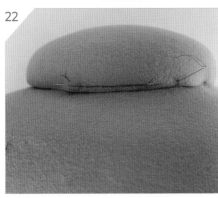

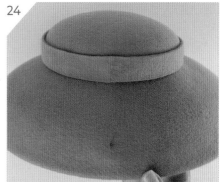

24. Check that it fits perfectly around the crown, cut the ends so they butt up together, then sew the ends together with a felt stab stitch. Brush over the join with a pin to hide it. Slide onto the crown and secure with three tie tacks (one at the CB and one on each side).

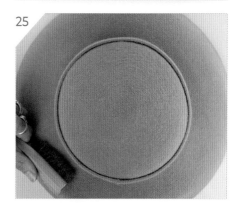

25. To give a neat finish to the hat, gently pass through steam and brush the felt with a wire brush or toothbrush in a clockwise motion, forming a circle in the middle. Support the hat with your other hand on the underside.

Making the felt flowers

26. Using the patterns from the Versatile Rose (see p. 152), cut the following: (note: grain line markings not required for felt)

small flower: three small petals, one felt strip ⅕" x 4⅓" (0.5 x 11 cm)

large flower: three small petals, three medium petals, one felt strip ⅕" x 4⅓" (0.5 x 11 cm)

leaves: one small, two medium

27. Lightly steam one petal, then push into the base area with your fingers to form a curve. Use your other fingers to curl over the tips. Repeat with each petal (see

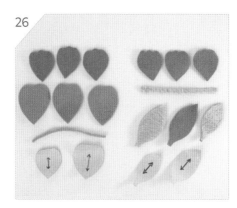

image). Lightly steam the leaves and form a curve in the ends with your fingers. The steam from an iron works well for this.

28. Tie a knot in the strips, then take a small petal and fold it around the knot. Sew together with a few stab stitches.

To construct the flowers, see step 10 (a, b, and c) of the Versatile Rose instructions (see p. 152).

29. Position the flowers and leaves onto the hat and secure using stab stitches. The flowers and lower leaf have been sewn through the brim, and the larger leaves through the base. The stitches on the underside should be invisible.

The hat has been finished with a lining and elastic (see pp. 126 and 130).

Tips
· The button block is used here as the crown, but it could be switched to a full crown block.

Why not try . . .
• switching the brim for a flat-patterned version, or finishing the brim edge by using petersham or fabric (see other projects).
• cutting the brim "raw" (if it is small) with no wire, folding, or binding. This gives a sharp, minimal finish.
• skipping the brim entirely and adding the flowers straight onto the base.

COUTURE FLAT PATTERNS
SCULPTING HEADWEAR WITHOUT A BLOCK

This chapter aims to open up a world of possibility through creating sculptural couture hats with flat patterns; no blocks required.

The techniques shown here are a mix between those used in traditional blocked hats and those used in "cut and sew" (soft fabric hats constructed with a sewing machine).

Making millinery in this way is not only great for beginners but for the more advanced too, since your designs can be led by your imagination rather than your equipment. You can create dramatic sculptural shapes of any size, altering them as often as you like with no commitment to finding a suitable block. The only thing that can't be achieved is a curve within the surface of the material (for example, if you wanted a bowler hat crown or an upsweep brim); for this, an element of blocking is required. However, some curving can be created by using the free-form hand-shaping techniques detailed throughout the book.

The methods in this chapter can also be blended with those covered in the blocking section—for example, a flat-patterned shape could be used as a trim on a blocked base, or a blocked crown could be paired with a flat-pattern brim. Flat patterns are also a great way to incorporate small pieces of materials and limit waste.

The Mixed-Media Headpiece in the next chapter uses this method.

Flat-pattern tips
When using buckram, try to keep it rolled rather than folded to avoid getting creases, which can be hard to completely remove without wetting.

You can copy these patterns to create these projects in their entirety, or experiment with your own. Play around with cutting and taping together card to build shapes and pin them to a mannequin head or block. Taking photos of the shape as it changes is useful, in case you like something you have taken apart.

Hand-Shaped Felt Saucer

MATERIALS

- felt hood; here I have used wool, but fur will give a higher-quality look and stretches easier.
- minimum 45¼" (115 cm) no. 3 petersham (amounts may differ depending on the end size of your hat)
- 65" (165 cm) strong millinery wire—minimum 35½" (90 cm) for hat, and 29⅓" (74.5 cm) for Alice band
- 3 quills
- nail polish
- matching thread
- 2" x 35½" (5 x 90 cm) strip of stretchy tulle for the Alice band

EQUIPMENT

- sewing kit
- bowl of water / water spray
- iron
- kettle/steamer
- clean, small paintbrush
- scalpel & cutting mat
- ruler
- pressing cloth (thick cloth or dishcloth)
- wire cutters / pliers
- clothes pegs
- curling tongs to shape quills (alternative equipment can be used; see p. 116)
- mannequin (optional)
- stiffener

A dramatic yet wearable hat for special occasions

Flattening the felt hood

1. Make a cut from the edge of the felt toward the tip of the hood, stopping just before the curve of the tip.

1

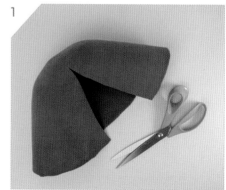

2. Starting at the corner of the cut and the outer edge, work on a section of felt the length of your iron. Soak the pressing cloth, then press the iron down onto the felt for a few seconds, so steam works itself into the felt, making a sizzling sound, and it becomes malleable. You can fold back the other corner for easier access..

3. Working quickly while the fabric is steaming, pull and stretch the felt outward along the edge. Use the cooler part of the cloth to cover your hand to pull, since the felt can get quite hot. Pull as hard as you can, and hold the felt until it stops steaming and cools slightly. If you let go too soon, the felt will shrink back to its original shape.

4. Repeat this, working around the edge to the other corner, then go inward a little and work around again. The aim is to keep expanding the edge and in toward the center to eventually create a flat shape. Snip farther into the tip if required, but don't go farther than the center, since the surface area you are left with will be too small to cut a circle from. The process may need to be repeated a few times, especially with wool felts, since they are much stiffer than fur. As the shape becomes flatter, use your arms to hold the felt in place and push upward and outward on the felt to stretch it in both directions.

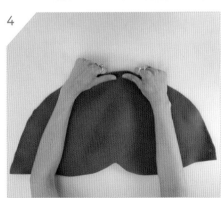

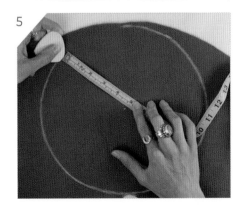

Gradually reduce the amount of moisture on the cloth as the felt becomes flatter—this helps it dry quicker and reduces the amount of shrinkage as it dries.

Leave the felt to completely dry, then stiffen. It is better to stiffen now rather than prior to stretching, since the stiffener makes the stretching process more difficult. Once the stiffener is dry, press again with a dry cloth and steam to work the stiffener in and further flatten the shape.

Drawing the patterns

5. The felt is now ready to be cut. The shape and size of your circle will be determined by your flattened felt. I have sewn a tie tack in the center of the felt, then measured out and marked the line with chalk, but you could use a pair of compasses, a plate, or something similar.

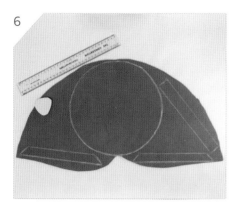

6. From the remaining felt, draw one long rectangle and two smaller rectangles the same size, with angled ends. Make sure the lines are straight and even. Again these will be determined by what you have.

Cutting the pieces out

7. Press firmly with a sharp scalpel and keep it at the same angle throughout the whole process so the cut line is even, especially on the strips of felt, since these edges won't be covered and it's easy to end up with a wobbly line. Cut against a ruler for the straight edges (see image). Imperfect edges can be remedied to an extent by softening the edge with sandpaper, and any remaining chalk can be dusted off.

Fitting the wire edge

8. Measure the circumference of the circle of felt and add 2" (5 cm) to this measurement. Cut a length of strong millinery wire to this length, then de-spring and shape the wire to fit the felt edge and bind the join (see p. 28).

9. Sew to the edge with wire stitch.

Attaching the petersham edge

10. Iron the petersham under a cloth if it is crinkled, then press along the length with your fingers to make a fold.

11. Starting just past the center of the wire join, pin the petersham around the shape with the fold on the edge, keeping it as taut as possible. Upon reaching the end, bring the petersham over the starting point of the petersham, then cut it so it overlaps by ³⁄₅" (1.5 cm). Fold under this end by ¹⁄₅" (0.5 cm) and pin down.

12. Secure the ribbon in place with a tacking stitch.

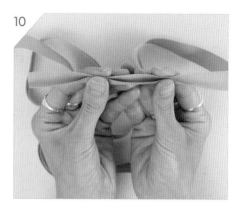

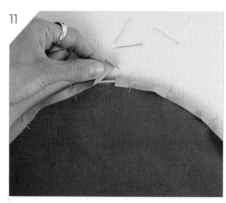

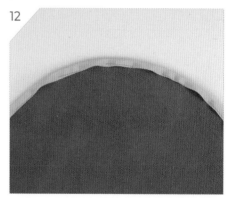

13. Hide your knot under the petersham, then sew the petersham down by using stab stitch, angling the needle diagonally forward with each stitch. Try to stitch inside the little scalloped edges in the ribbon, each stitch roughly four loops apart.

14. Using a clean brush, paint the petersham with boiling water to shrink any puckers into a perfect shape. Apply quickly and evenly to ensure no watermarks appear.

Compiling the trim

15. While the petersham is drying, take the longer felt strip, draw a "V" shape on the ends, and cut with the scalpel.

16. Cut a new length of petersham that is ³⁄₅" (1.5 cm) longer than this felt strip. Fold over the end by roughly 3 mm, then fold the corners inward.

17. Pin the petersham along one edge of the felt as before, and pin the folded petersham end neatly over the tip. Repeat with the other end. Stab-stitch together.

18. Dampen the pressing cloth and use it to make a lengthways fold in the felt strip. Hold it for a moment so it stays in place.

19. Tie this into a knot. If it's a bit stiff, guide it through steam first.

20. Bring together the ends of the two remaining felt strips and whipstitch them at the top and bottom to create points.

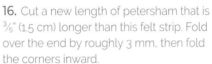

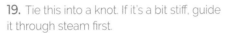

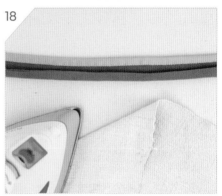

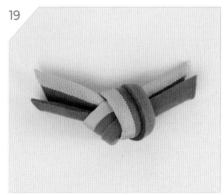

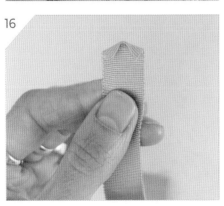

21. Bring the top and bottom points together, then place the knot on top. Pin all the pieces to secure, then stab-stitch together. Try to keep the stitches to the back of the knot, and use pliers to pull the needle through if it's difficult to grasp.

22. Prepare the quills. The edges of curling tongs have been used to shape the wider part of these, then the tips have been curled around the tongs. They have then been painted with a gold nail polish at the base and pink on the tips (see p. 116 for more on working with quills).

Shaping the saucer

23. Shape a gentle curve at the middle points on both sides with your hands, positioning the join just below the curve on the right-hand side; this will be the least visible point on the hat.

24. Now face the saucer with the curved sides facing away, keeping the join on your right. The top and bottom areas should face toward you. Bend another gentle curve, as shown. This curve will frame the face at the front.

Check in the mirror or on a mannequin that you like the shape, then add a pin where the saucer sits at the CF, so you remember the positioning.

Assembling the pieces

Make a tulle-covered Alice band (see p. 127).

25. Place the Alice band on the mannequin or your head (a mannequin is easier), and position the saucer. Feel the Alice band under the felt and choose two points along the front of the saucer that touch the Alice band, roughly 2¾" (7 cm) apart. Place pins at these points, then do the same on the back wire, roughly 1⅕" (3 cm) apart. Lift up the saucer and add pins in the Alice band at the same points. Then pin the Alice band to the underside of the

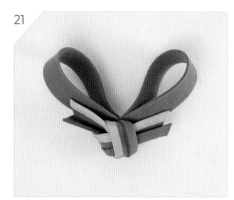

21

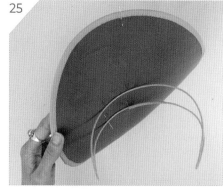

25

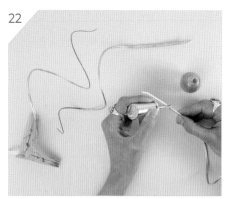

22

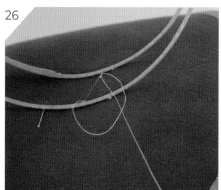

26

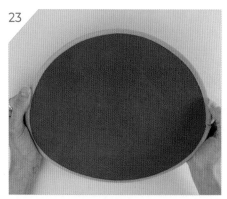

23

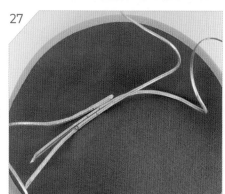

27

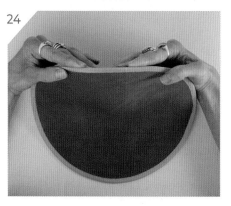

24

felt at these points. This can be fiddly, but try to wriggle the pins through the tulle and into the felt. It shouldn't wobble but also shouldn't distort the shape of the felt.

26. Check the position again, then stitch between these points, stab-stitching back and forth through the felt and tulle.

27. Now position the quills and pin in place through their sides. Each quill will need to be attached in two locations roughly ⅘" (2 cm) apart. Try to keep the attachment areas of all quills in the same place so they can be hidden under the felt knot. Sew through each quill three or four times so they don't wobble (see pp. 117 and 118).

Now position, pin, and sew the felt knot in at least three locations, stab-stitching a few times through the saucer and the parts of the knot closest to it. You may need to tie off your thread and restart at each place.

Why not try . . .
• making the saucer from sinamay by ironing flat and stiffening three layers of sinamay, using the method from the halo (see p. 72). You could make the saucer any shape and size you wish, and finish the edge like the halo, or with petersham.
• adding a small base under the saucer and using elastic instead of an Alice band.

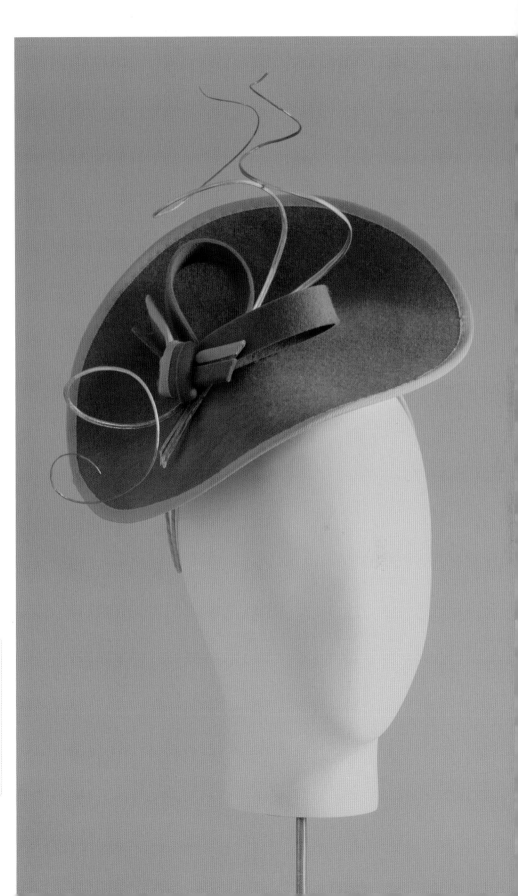

Sinamay and Organdie Halo Hair Band

MATERIALS
- 17¾" x 17¾" (45 x 45 cm) sinamay
- 32" (81 cm) strong millinery wire
- 23½" x 11⅞" (60 x 30 cm) piece of organdie fabric
- matching thread

EQUIPMENT
- sewing kit
- matching flat-tipped marker pen
- iron
- pencil or tailor's chalk
- wire cutters / pliers
- pressing cloth (organza or organdie)
- hair band and trim paper patterns (see p. 154)
- kettle/steamer
- stiffener

A versatile accessory, adaptable for daytime, parties, or formal events

Making the hair band

1. Prepare the paper patterns and put the trim patterns aside. Iron the sinamay flat, then pin the hair band pattern to the sinamay on the bias. Using a sharp pencil or chalk, carefully draw around the pattern, then remove the pattern and cut out. Produce two of these on the bias, then one on the straight of grain.

1

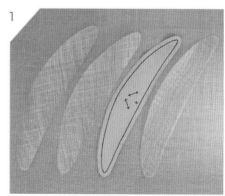

2. Despring and roughly flatten the wire, then shape it so it fits perfectly around the inner line of the pattern, with a 2" (5 cm) overlap to one side of the bottom edge (see image).

Color the wire, using a flat-tipped marker to match the sinamay so the wire is not seen, (see p. 126). Then bind the wire overlap (see p. 28).

3. Take one bias cut piece of sinamay and the straight cut piece. Place the straight cut piece on top of the other, and iron them to seal them together through a pressing cloth. If your sinamay isn't prestiffened, they won't stick, so add a little stiffener first, then iron once dry.

4. Place the wire on top of the shape so it fits in the same position as the inner line on the paper pattern. Pin in place, then sew with a wire stitch.

5. Fold the double layer of sinamay over the wire with your fingers; dampen your fingers to fold in the corners so the sinamay doesn't break.

6. Steam-iron it on a flat surface to form a crisp edge.

7. Trim off any uneven edges so it looks neat and even.

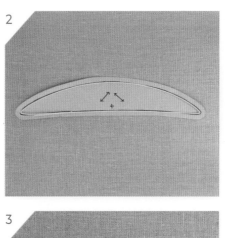

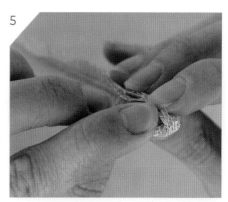

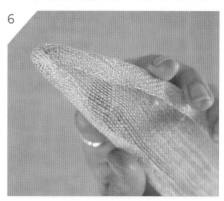

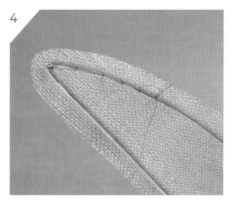

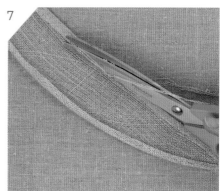

8. Use the tacking stitch to secure the last sinamay layer on top of the other two, sandwiching the wire inside.

9. Fold the edges of the single layer inward in the same way as the other layer; the folded line should sit neatly along the existing edge. Wet your fingers slightly if the sinamay feels brittle.

10. Trim back the folded edge in the same way as before.

11. Stab-stitch the layers together. The tacking stitches can now be removed.

12. With the double layer facing outward to the front, hold the corners and gently bend the wire to form a smooth curve. You'll need to use extra pressure on the wire join. Keep bending with a light touch until you achieve a head-shaped curve that is comfortable to wear. The flat edge is the edge that will sit on the head.

Preparing the trim

13. Pin on, draw around, and cut out five leaves and three rose patterns from the organdie. Follow the layout in the image to use the fabric economically.

14. Paint a thin line of stiffener along the edges of each piece, no more than ⅖" (1 cm) wide. The straight bottom edges of the rose patterns won't need stiffening.

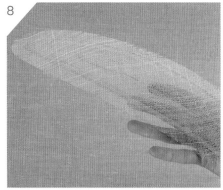

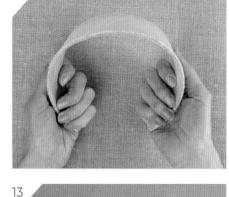

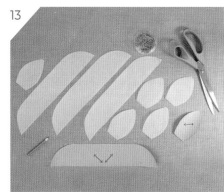

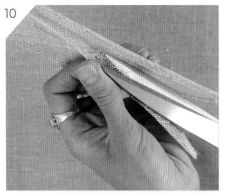

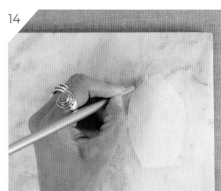

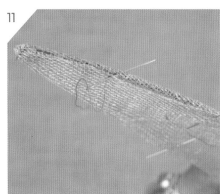

Rolling the edges

15. Once dry, take one of the organdie shapes. Starting at a bottom corner, create a tiny fold along the very edge of one side with your fingers, then carry this on around the whole shape. Note: the straight line of the rose pattern and the base of the leaves don't need to be rolled. Start at the base of each leaf and work toward the tips.

16. Now, starting in the same place as above, dampen the tips of your index/ middle fingers and thumbs (I dip them in a dish of water, then dab off the excess on a cloth). Pull the edge of the organdie taut between these fingers. Begin pushing the edge back and forth until it starts to curl over and the raw edge is concealed inside the roll, making the roll as tight as possible. Work around the shape, edging along slowly, dampening your fingers when they dry. You're aiming for a tight, even roll. You can go along the shape again if required, since it can take a few attempts to get it straight. The roll should contain just under $2/5$" (1 cm) of fabric. You can try rolling with your fingers on top as in the previous image, or your thumbs.

Repeat steps 15 and 16 for each of the roses and the leaves.

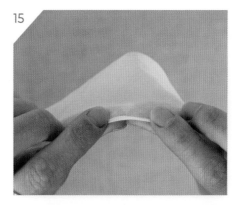

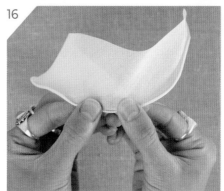

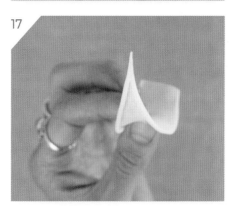

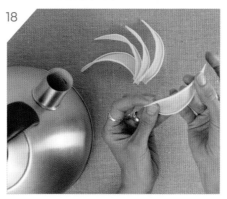

Finishing the tips of the leaves

17. This part of the leaves is more difficult to refine, since the weave becomes straighter and the fabric strip is thinner and needs to be formed into a point, so take your time. Roll one edge over the other, until you get a sharp point.

Setting the shape

18. Prepare your steam. Hold on to the leaf by the base and guide it quickly through the steam, keeping your fingers away from the steam. Then hold it gently by the point and base, curving it over your fingers so it is slightly taut for ten to fifteen seconds, until it sets. This neatens the shape and sets the roll (see image). Set each leaf, then guide the rose pieces through, holding on to each end. The curved ends here are also tricky to get a smooth roll; pulling them tight and rerolling back and forth will help.

Making the bias roses

19. Sew a running stitch along the straight bottom edges. The stitch length should be roughly ⅖" (1 cm). ⅕" (0.5 cm) from the bottom. Leave the needle attached to the thread.

20. Loosely gather the fabric and begin rolling the strip to form the rose. This can be quite fiddly so will take a little practice. The roll will need fewer gathers in the center for the bud area, and more as the petals become more open. If you would like younger-looking roses, use fewer gathers; more-mature flowers, add more gathers. Hold on to the base of the rose and the thread as you go around, since it's easy for the center to slip out and gathers to undo as you are concentrating on forming the shape.

21. Using the needle still attached to the thread, stab-stitch through the layers a few times in different directions, then tie off to secure.

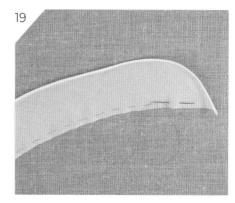

19

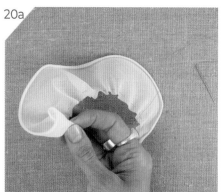

20a

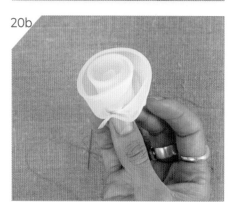

20b

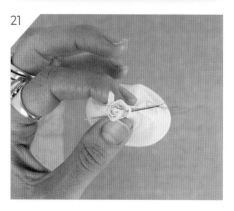

21

22. Stab-stitch two roses together at their bases, then add the third. Make sure they are compact and not too splayed out. Sew through the outer "petals" slightly higher than the base to draw them together. Next, pinch the base of a leaf, then pin on and sew this to the base of the roses.

23. Check the shape on the halo, then position, pin, and sew the remaining leaves.

24. Position and pin the trim onto the side of the headband, using tie tacks in a number of locations to secure it enough that it doesn't move around. Hide all tie tack knots behind the trim around the base. If you would like to hold any leaves in place, tie-tack them to the halo, sewing under the rolled edges and making sure the stitches don't pull them out of shape.

22

23

24

Why not try . . .
• stretching the sinamay on the bias before cutting out the patterns (for a more dense-looking hair band).
• changing the back section of the halo to a contrasting color.
• making it out of stiffened, flattened felt with a petersham bind.

Fabric-Covered Wide-Brim Boater

A striking wide-brimmed style based on the traditional boater

Made to a 22" (56 cm) head fitting.

MATERIALS

- 39" (1 m) of 59" (150 cm) wide duchess satin
- 23½" (60 cm) of 43⅓" (110 cm) wide black or white buckram
- 23½" (60 cm) of 59" (150 cm) wide lightweight domette
- 78¾" (2 m) adhesive webbing
- 78¾" (2 m) strong millinery wire
- 25½" x 4¾" (65 x 12 cm) bias strip of sinamay
- 7⅞" (20 cm) square duchess satin for the bow
- matching thread
- 23" (58 cm) no. 5 petersham
- lining fabric (see p. 130)

EQUIPMENT

- sewing kit
- buckram pressing cloth (organza or organdie)
- top fabric-pressing cloth (organza or organdie)
- tailor's chalk or pencil
- iron
- small clips/pegs
- wire cutters / pliers
- paper patterns (tip, side band, brim, hatband, bow loop, bow; pp. 149–151)
- fabric glue

Preparing the base materials

1. Prepare the paper patterns. Put the hatband, bow loop, and bow pieces aside.

Protect the ironing board with a cloth, then iron flat the buckram under a pressing cloth. It may need a little steam if it is very creased.

Pin the brim, tip, and side band patterns to the buckram (see image).

1

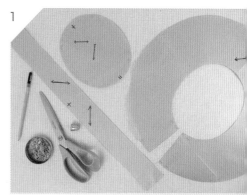

2. Using a sharp pencil or chalk, carefully transfer the patterns on to the buckram, including the CF and CB on the tip, and the CF on the brim and side band. Do so by lifting the edge of the pattern and marking a cross for the CF and two lines for the CB.

Remove the paper and cut out the buckram.

3. Now transfer and cut the patterns in domette and adhesive webbing. Place your patterns economically to make sure you don't waste fabric.

You will need these:
domette: one tip, one side band, two brims

adhesive webbing: two tips, two side bands, four brims (the webbing doesn't need to be cut on the bias, since it has no weave)

Lay out one of each of the three materials for the tip, side band, and brim.

Sandwich the adhesive webbing between the corresponding buckram and domette pieces, with the domette on top. Align them accurately, matching up all markings (see image).

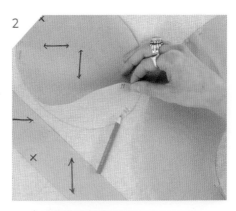

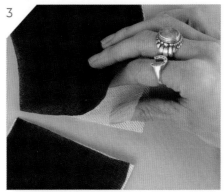

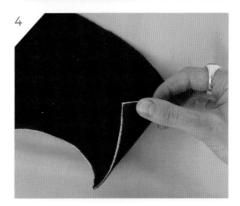

4. On a medium heat setting, dry-iron the domette until it fuses securely to the buckram on each pattern piece. Use gentle pressure and do not drag the fabric, since this can distort the shape and cause it to buckle.

Next, take the second domette brim piece and another of the webbing, turn the brim over, and repeat the process so the domette is fused on both sides of the brim.

Cutting the satin

5. With the satin facing right side down, pin on and transfer the paper patterns as economically as possible, leaving around 1¾" (4.5 cm) of space between each piece, keeping them in one corner (the remainder of the fabric will be needed for a long bias strip 47⅗" x 1½" [121 x 4 cm]). Lift up the front of the paper to mark on the CF and CB with chalk as before. You will need one tip, one side band, and two brims. Note: only one is shown here for demonstration.

6. Cut the pieces out, leaving approx. ⅘" (2 cm) extra around the edges of each piece. The outer edge of the brim doesn't need this seam allowance but can be cut on the pattern line. On the satin brim pieces, cut through the center of the fabric at the CB.

Put the tip, side band, and second brim piece aside.

Constructing the brim

7. Lay out the domette-covered buckram brim piece. Lay the second adhesive webbing on top, then satin on top of this (right side up), making sure they are perfectly aligned.

Using a clean pressing cloth, iron the satin to fuse the layers. Press gently without moving the iron, and take care it doesn't scorch the satin. Steady the fabric with your other hand to help avoid stretching and causing uneven distribution of fabric, since it will cause the buckram layer to buckle or fabric to crinkle once stuck together.

8. Turn over the brim and repeat the process with the final satin and webbing pieces, but this time leave ⅗" (1.5 cm) of the CB seam unironed on each side.

9. On the outer edge of the brim, trim back any satin or domette edges that spill over the buckram.

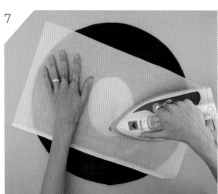

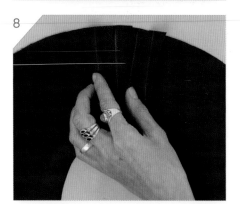

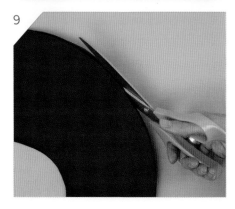

10. Create tabs at the headline. Snip into the satin at ⅗" (1.5 cm) intervals, leaving roughly 2 mm uncut toward the buckram headline.

Joining the brim CB seam

11. At the CB, trim the satin seam allowance to around ⅖" (1 cm) on both sides, then fold the excess satin from the top side around to the underside (the underside has the ⅗" [1.5 cm] section unstuck). With a small amount of glue, stick the folded pieces underneath and hold until the glue has set.

12. Turn over the brim so the topside faces up, and join the edges by pinning along the seam.

13. Squeeze the join in one hand and slip-stitch the seam.

14. Turn the brim over to the underside, then fold under the ⅖" (1 cm) satin seam allowance so the joins match without any sag and resemble the top seam you have just sewn. Glue down the folds (see image).

Pin and slip-stitch together like the other side. (You can add some glue under the join once sewn if it looks "loose." Do so by putting a small amount of glue on the tip of a needle and sliding it inside the layers from the outer edge.)

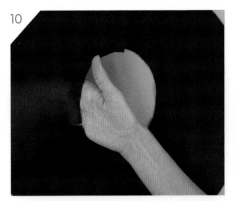

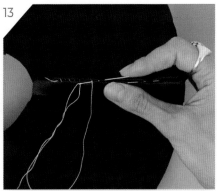

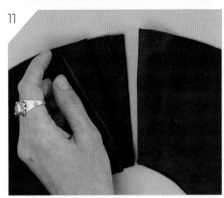

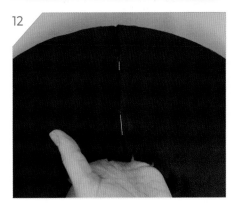

Wiring the pattern pieces

15. Measure out two lengths of wire, one 51⅗" (131 cm) for the brim and one 24⅕" (61.5 cm) for the tip. Despring and roughly flatten the wire (see p. 28).

Shape the wires so they fit around the brim and tip paper patterns. Shape so each has a 2" (5 cm) overlap at CB. It is easier to shape them on top of the paper patterns since they are flat. However, you'll need to tweak the brim wire so it fits perfectly around the fabric brim once a smooth shape has been formed on the paper (see image).

Position the wires on top of the fabric pieces to check they fit. The wires should fit just on the inside edge. If the wire doesn't sit perfectly here, you will encounter problems when you come to the last stage of attaching it, and it will need to be remade.

16. Once you are happy with the fit, bind the overlaps. Place joins at the CB, then secure into place with clips or pegs. Check again that the wire fits well.

Using the wire stitch, sew the wires on. Start at the CB and remove pegs as you go. Secure the last stitch just over your first.

15
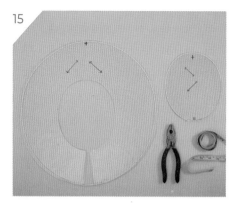

16
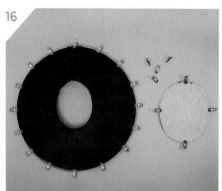

17

18

Making the brim bias binding

17. Cut a bias strip of satin 47⅗" (121 cm) long and 1½" (4 cm) wide. Bring the two ends together with the right sides of fabric facing in. Sew ⅖" (1 cm) from the ends, using a backstitch, and iron open the seam.

18. Place the brim facing right way up and lay the bias strip around the outer brim edge, with its right side facing the brim. Matching the CBs and raw edges together, pin the strip around the wired edge, sliding your pins gently through the top surfaces and over the wire. Pin at N–S, E–W positions to distribute the strip evenly around the shape.

19. Secure by sewing ⅖" (1 cm) in from the edge with a backstitch going through all layers, or with a sewing-machine straight stitch.

20. Roll the bias strip over the wired edge, then fold under the raw edges as tightly as possible. The fold should cover over the existing stitches. Pin in place and slip-stitch to secure, taking your needle through the satin layers only. Use pliers to pull your needle through if it becomes too fiddly to grasp it firmly.

The petersham head ribbon can now be added to the head fitting (see p. 30).

Preparing the side band
21. Take all three of the side band materials, then sandwich the adhesive webbing between the satin and domette and carefully iron to fuse together as before. Fold the excess fabric over the top and bottom edges and glue to the underside of the buckram, then do the same with the ends, trimming off excess bulk.

22. Pin, then slip-stitch the ends together.

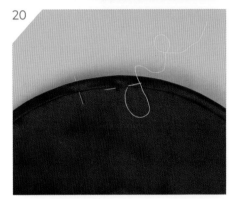

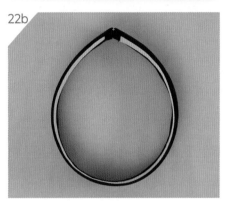

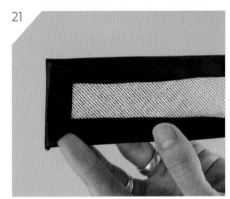

Constructing the crown

23. Complete the tip by fusing the satin piece to the domette, using the webbing as before. Carefully snip into the satin seam allowance at ⅗" (1.5 cm) intervals, creating tabs. Leave around 3 mm uncut so it can be turned under and glued.

24. Lay the paper pattern back onto the tip and use as a guide to slide pins into the satin at the CB and CF positions. Remove the paper pattern. Matching up the CBs and CFs, ease the tip into the side band and pin together. Angle the pins down through the tip into the side band. The tip should sit just inside the top edge of the side band. Take time to align these neatly and securely.

25. Slip-stitch the tip and side band together around the join, catching the satin layers only. Start by bringing your first stitch up from inside at the CB, and finish by taking it back down inside to tie off. This is now your crown.

26. Pin the crown to the brim, matching up CBs and working the pins around in N–S, E–W, etc. Due to the thickness of the fabric, it is easier to position the pins horizontally rather than across. However, be careful not to scratch your hands in the next step.

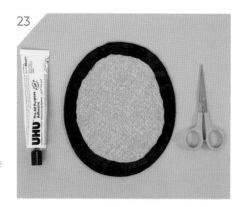

27. Using double thread, sew together roughly ⅕" (0.5 cm) above the join with a backstitch.

Constructing the hatband

28. Iron the bias strip of sinamay, pulling it as you go to take out the stretch.

29. Pin the hatband pattern on to the sinamay, mark, and cut.

Fold into thirds lengthways, finger pressing as you go (see image), then iron. You can fold the pattern along the dotted line and place it in the middle of the strip as a guide to help achieve a straight edge if required.

30. On the remaining sinamay, prepare the hatband "bow loop" pattern piece in the same way as above to create a short folded strip. Bend this strip into thirds to create a loop, then backstitch together. It should be the same width as the hatband.

27

31. Slide the "bow loop" onto the hatband, then bring the ends of the hatband together. Sew together with backstitch, leaving a $^2/_5$" (1 cm) seam allowance. Press the seam open. Make sure all the raw edges and seams are on the same side; this will be the inside (see image).

Turn the hatband out the right way if required, trim any rough strands from the hatband, join, and slide the "bow loop" over the join.

30

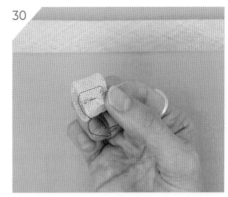

Making the bow
32. Pin, mark, and cut out the bow pattern. Fold down the center of the fabric pattern piece with the right sides inward, and backstitch using small stitches around the edge (this can also be stitched on a machine). Leave one of the small edges free to turn out the shape.

31

28

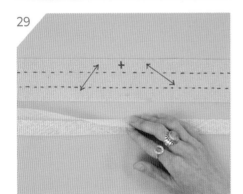

29

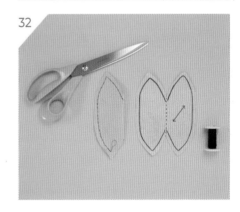

32

33. Trim the pointed tips and turn out. Ease out the tips gently with a pin.

Pinch the center of the bow until you find a shape you like. Pin it, then stitch it in place with a tie tack.

34. Wiggle the bow through the bow loop, then stitch together, hiding stitches by sewing around the back of the bow and under the bow loop.

33

34

35

35. Slide the hatband over the crown, positioning the bow where you like. Secure with tie tacks along the bottom edge of the hatband, tying them on the inside of the hat under the petersham. Don't pull too tight, since this will cause puckers in the fabric. Two or three will be enough—one under the bow, one on the opposite side, and one at the back. Avoid adding one at the front, since the eye will be drawn to it.

Add a lining (see p. 130) and elastic (see p. 126).

Why not try . . .
· using the crown on its own as a pillbox, by wiring the bottom edge, turning the fabric under, and adding a lining.
· altering the patterns to create different-shaped designs—shorter brims, taller crowns, etc.
· shrinking the patterns for a mini version.
· cutting the top fabric with the straight of grain at the front. I prefer the bias since it gives a softer feel to the design.

Tips
· Adhesive spray can be used instead of adhesive webbing, great for bonding fabrics to buckram around curved shapes.

SUSTAINABILITY
LIMITING WASTE, REPURPOSING, AND UPCYCLING

Making your own millinery and moving through a careful, considered process often leads to the creation of a treasured item. It is an alternative to the mass-produced, disposable market, and a place where less indeed means more. Lovers of couture millinery tend to appreciate the skill and time involved in a handmade product, and want to invest in an object of high quality.

The industry has come a long way since demand for rare and exotic plumage on hats led to many birds being hunted to extinction. In fact, some companies now offer cruelty-free feathers, rabbit fur felt as 100 percent byproduct, and vegan material options. Even some sheet plastics are now available 100 percent recycled, which are often a popular addition to modern designs.

Despite these progressions, many of the processes and materials used in millinery contribute to the strain on the environment, with the fashion and garment industry being a large part of the bigger problem. You may want to explore the origins of your choice of materials and their carbon footprint, ethical status, and long-term effects.

In this chapter we look at ways to limit waste by upcycling a preowned hat, repurposing a vintage treasure, and finding inventive ways to make the most of material remnants.

Some ideas to consider
• Swapping trims can be a great way to refresh hats, instead of making new pieces from scratch.
• Keep an eye out for beautiful fabrics in thrift stores, charity shops, or online. Repurposed fabric can be used for any of the fabric designs in this book.
• Unusual flowers can be created by mixing offcuts of fabric, creating interesting textures, patterns, and color combinations.
• A swap shop with fellow milliners could be a great way to share your unused materials and equipment.

Mixed-Media Headpiece

A fun, easy-to-wear, and adaptable party piece

MATERIALS
- 17⅓" (44 cm) medium/strong millinery wire
- 4¾" (12 cm) fine millinery wire
- 1⅕" x 16½" (3 x 42 cm) long bias strip of tarlatan and roughly 13" x 13" (33 x 33 cm) square of tarlatan (domette can also be used for extra thickness)
- 8¼" x 6" (21 x 15 cm) buckram
- 11⅖" x 6" (29 x 15 cm) piece of veiling
- 13" x 13" (33 x 33 cm) vintage fabric remnant
- mixed fabric remnants, large enough to fit the circle patterns (here I have used an upcycled PVC shower curtain, veiling, sinamay, and recycled paper)
- hat elastic

EQUIPMENT
- sewing kit
- pressing cloth (organza/organdie)
- wire cutters / pliers
- tailor's chalk / pencil
- water misting bottle (or the spray feature on some irons)
- clips or pegs
- bradawl (optional)
- iron
- base and 2 circle paper patterns (see p. 153)

In millinery, it is not always possible to buy local. For example, sinamay is produced from the abaca plant, grown and woven only in the Philippines. With the distance many materials travel, it's worth finding ways to use every piece. Here we use various recycled remnants for the trim and vintage fabric for the base, which not only helps reduce waste but can add value by making a piece limited edition or a "one-off."

Preparing the base materials

1.   Iron flat the buckram under the cloth. If your buckram is folded, it will need extra ironing and possible steam to remove creases.

Pin the pattern onto the buckram, matching up the arrows with grain lines to ensure the pattern is positioned on the bias in the most economical way you can. Draw around with chalk or pencil, then remove the paper pattern and cut out the buckram shape.

Despring and roughly flatten the wire (see p. 28). Shape the wire so it fits perfectly on the edge of the buckram shape with approx. 2" (5 cm) overlap at the back, then bind the overlap.

2. Sew the wire onto the underside edge of the buckram, using wire stitch (the side of the pattern without markings).

3. With the wire on the bottom of the shape, gently bend the shape along the front edge to give it an even, head-shaped curve, then do the same with the back. You'll need some direct pressure with your thumbs on the wire join since this is harder to shape.

4. Lay the paper pattern onto the tarlatan, ensuring the bias is correctly positioned. Pin, mark with chalk, then cut out.

Place the vintage top fabric with its wrong side facing up and draw on the pattern, then add an additional $\frac{4}{5}$" (2 cm) seam allowance all around before cutting. You can draw this on or cut by eye. Flip the paper pattern over and cut another with $\frac{4}{5}$" (2 cm) seam allowance from the vintage fabric (this piece will be used to line the headpiece on the underside). Remove the paper pattern. The reversed vintage fabric piece can be put aside.

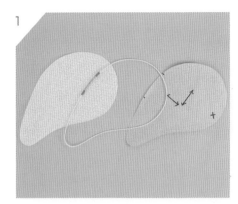

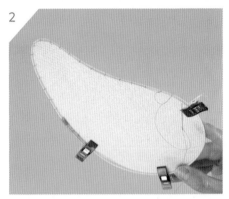

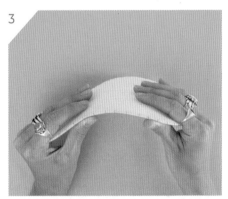

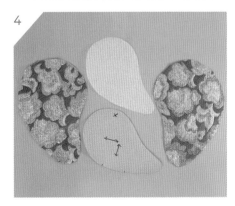

5. Place the tarlatan over the wired buckram, matching up the shapes, then spritz with a very small amount of fine water mist on half the shape. Cover your hand with a cloth or press pad. With the tip of a medium-heated iron, gently press down the tarlatan, moving the iron in the direction of the fabric weave so it doesn't buckle. The tarlatan should begin fusing to the buckram. If it's too wet, the tarlatan will stick to the iron and the buckram will become soft. You may want to try practicing on some remnants first.

6. Take the bias strip of tarlatan. Pin the end of the tarlatan ⅖" (1 cm) over the CB, then pull the tarlatan around the shape so it stretches into the curves and folds itself evenly over the edge. The tarlatan should fit smoothly around the shape. Hold in place with clips or pegs.

7. Fold over the other end at the CB, overlapping by ⅖" (1 cm), then trim off any excess. Sew down with a backstitch.

8. Position the vintage fabric over the base, then pin to the underside of the base by pulling evenly and working in N–S, E–W positions. Start by pinning on the straight of grain. **(image a)**

Pins spaced roughly ⅘" (2 cm) apart will be fine, although you will probably need more at the pointed end. **(image b)**

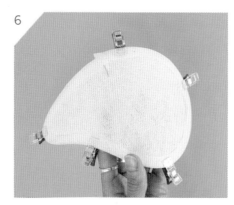

6

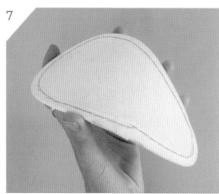

7

8a

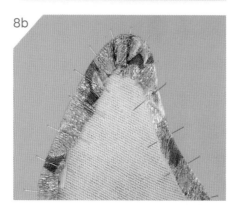

8b

9. Once smooth, sew the top fabric to the tarlatan, using a diagonal running stitch. Trim back any excess fabric to remove bulk.

10. Add a small outward curve to the pointed end of the base.

Constructing the pompom
11. Using the circle patterns, cut the following amount from the material remnants, or use your own combination. You may find you need a few more circles if your fabric is finer or has less structure.

Small circle:
6 sinamay
3 vinyl
3 recycled paper
3 adhesive webbing

Large circle:
3 veiling

12. Sandwich the adhesive webbing between three of the sinamay circles and the paper circles, and iron until they fuse.

9

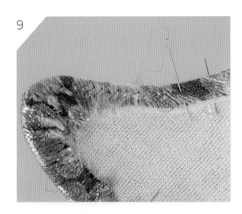

13. Now fold a circle in half, slightly over the center point, then pinch it at the base and form a ripple.

14. Sew through the pinched point twice, then tie the ends. Repeat this with all the circles.

15. Take the 4¾" (12 cm) length of fine millinery wire and bend a small loop into the top. Twist the end around the length to secure.

16. Sew the base of one circle through the loop in the wire, sliding it between a fold in the base. Use a few stitches so it doesn't slide around, then tie off to secure.

13

10

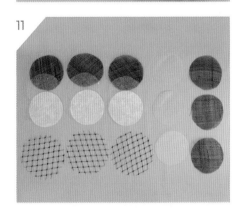

14

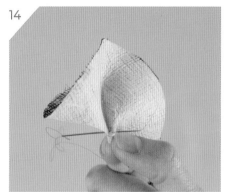

11

15

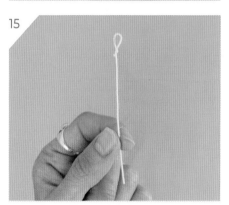

12

16

17. Keep adding circles, making sure the range of materials is evenly dispersed. You can use a single piece of thread for a few circles but will need to knot the thread near the base of the pompom and start with a new piece. As you add more circles, this becomes more fiddly, but keep an eye on the shape and arrangement as you go to ensure your pompom stays relatively round.

18. Take the rectangle of veiling and gather it in the center with your hands, then pin the gather to the base, roughly one-third of the way up from the pointed end. Sew to the base with a few stitches.

19. Make a small hole next to the place the veiling has been sewn. This can be done with a piece of strong wire, with a bradawl, or carefully with the point of some small scissors, just big enough to poke the wire through. Poke the end of the pompom wire through the hole to a point where the pompom rests just above the base, then bend the wire into a curve that sits flat on the underside. Sew down with a wire stitch, going through to the base on the other side with a stab stitch.

17a

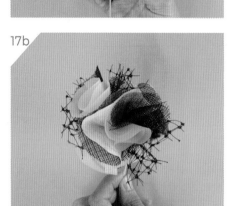

17b

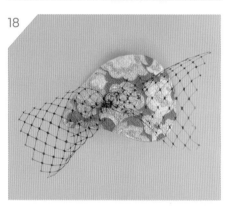

18

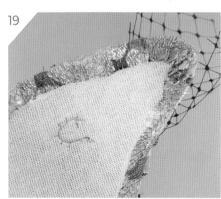

19

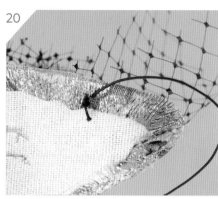

20

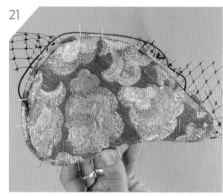

21

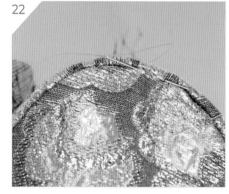

22

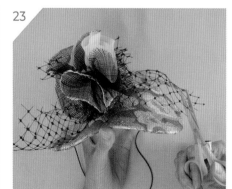

23

20. Attach a length of elastic to the base, in the positions marked on the paper pattern. Sew it to the fabric that is turned over to the underside (see p. 126).

21. Lay the second piece of vintage fabric onto the bottom of the base and keep in place with a few pins.

Work around the shape, folding under the raw edges and repinning, so the fabric sits neatly around the shape. Pin from the outer edge of the fold, through the fabric on the base, and up again into the fabric you are working on. Work the pins around in N–S, E–W, and trim back any excess fabric to avoid bulk.

22. Slip-stitch together, removing pins as you go. Once you reach the end, bury the knot under the fold.

23. Snip into the veiling to give it a random, soft finish.

Why not try . . .
· making some pompoms as a trim on a larger hat.
· using recycled buttons and beads for extra detail.
· using flattened felt remnants for the base, finishing the edge by folding or with petersham or fabric binds.

Patchwork Felt Pillbox

MATERIALS

- 3 lengths of medium/strong millinery wire—one at 16" (41 cm), 2 at 16¾" (42.5 cm)
- felt remnants (enough to cover the patterns)
- lining fabric
- matching thread
- elastic (see p. 126)
- 17¾" (45 cm) no.3 petersham ribbon

EQUIPMENT

- sewing kit
- button block
- tip and side band paper patterns (see pp. 155 and 156)
- sharp pencil or tailor's chalk
- bowl of water or water spray and dishcloth/cloth for wet-ironing felt
- iron
- scalpel
- wire cutters / pliers
- cutting mat
- ruler
- stiffener

A neat and simple shape that can be formal or frivolous, depending on how it's styled

Entire hats can be created by joining remnants of felt, either flat or part blocked. This pillbox has been made using patchworked felt pieces and the top of the button block. These patterns have been made to fit the button block with 6¼" (16 cm) diameter. You may need to adjust the scale of the patterns if your block varies much from this.

There is no weave to felt, so you can position patterns in the most economical way regardless of direction.

Preparing the wires

1. Shape the shorter wire to fit around the oval-tip paper pattern, with a 2" (5cm) overlap. Shape the two longer wires so they fit snugly around the smaller wire. Bind the overlaps (see p. 28 for wire instruction).

Blocking the tip

2. Block a remnant of felt over the top of your button block; it needs to cover enough of the surface so the smaller wire oval can fit on top. Leave to dry. (See the blocking chapter from p. 36 for further instruction.)

Creating the side band

3. The side band pattern now needs to be cut into pieces; it's a good idea to color and number the pattern before cutting, to work out your color scheme and avoid confusion. Make sure you have enough of each color of felt to complete the design.

4. Your felt may already be stiffened from a previous project, but if not, stiffen the pieces on the side that you intend for the underside, (see p. 14 for stiffening). Once they are dry, iron them under the damp cloth to work in the stiffener.

Use a sharp pencil (or tailor's chalk for black) to mark the shapes onto the felt, then cut on the inside of the line. They need to be as precise as possible. Use sharp scissors or a scalpel.

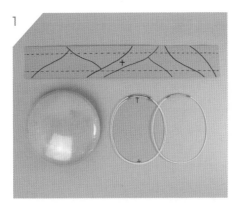

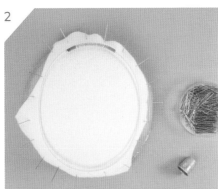

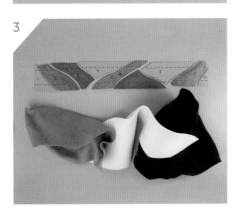

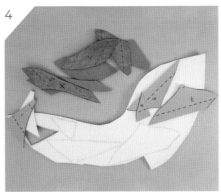

5. Lay out the pieces in order. Pin the first piece to the second and join with a felt stab stitch (see image). Join each section to the next, working along the line.

6. Last, join the CB seam in the same way.

7. Pin one of the larger wires inside the felt side band, at a distance of ⅗" (1.5 cm) from the edge. Use the "wire stitch in a fold" stitch to secure. Repeat with the second matching wire on the other edge.

8. Using the edge of a dampened cloth, press gently on a small section on one edge of the felt, just on and above the wire line.

9. Remove the cloth and fold the edge over the wire. The felt needs to become sufficiently malleable to enable the seams to fold over the wire without opening. If this happens, squeeze the felt seam together as you fold it over. Hold each section for a few seconds until it stays in place. Work around the edges both top and bottom in the same way.

Iron on the inside of the folds to further flatten them.

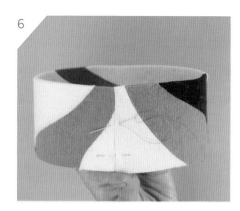

6

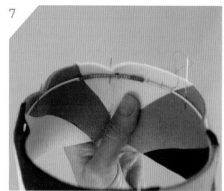

7

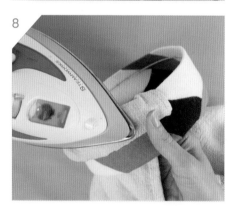

8

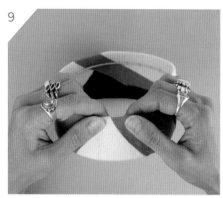

9

Creating the tip

10. Return to the blocked felt (if it is dry). Hold the wire oval down onto the block and draw around the outside.

11. Remove the felt from the block and cut out with sharp scissors. Position the wire oval on the underside of the felt and hold in place with clips, then sew down using the wire stitch.

12. Using the paper oval pattern as a guide, place pins at the CF and CB of the tip and side band.

13. Wiggle the tip into the side band, matching up the CF and CB pins. Pin the pieces together, working around in N–S, E–W positions.

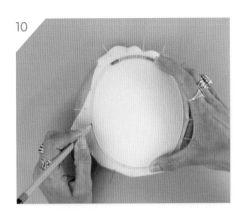

10

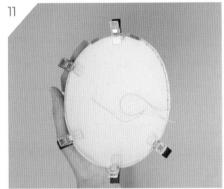

11

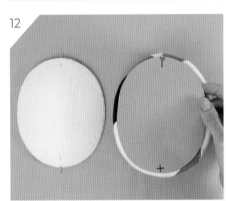

12

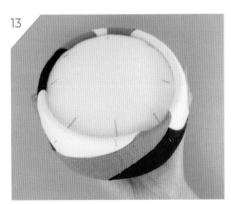

13

14. Stab-stitch together. Start by bringing the knotted thread up from inside the hat at the CB, and through the inner edge of the fold of the side band, then diagonally down through the edge of the tip section. Angle the needle back up and through to the inner edge of the fold again and repeat.

Sew in the petersham (see p. 30).

15. Cut eight thin strips of felt, roughly 4 mm wide and 8⅔" (22 cm) long, using a scalpel and ruler on the cutting mat. I have used four colors, adding a dusky-pink color to the three used in the hat.

16. Bring together the ends of four strips and stitch through them a few times to join. **(image a)** Repeat on the other end, then bring the ends together and join in the same way. **(image b)**

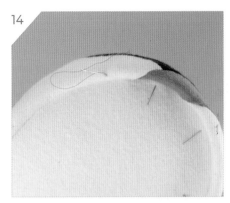

14

15

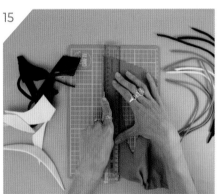

16a

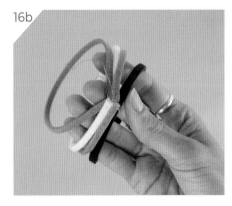

16b

17. Next, stitch the loop together in the middle to form a figure eight.

18. Take three more strips and stitch their centers to the center of the figure eight, then wrap the final strip around the center to conceal all the stitches. Stab-stitch this at the back, then cut the ends so they lie neatly.

19. Position and pin the bow over to the left side of the CF, and stab-stitch through the entire bow to the underside of the base, until it feels secure. Tie off the thread in a hidden location.

20. Tie-tack the front strips to the hat so they complement the lines of the patchwork, then snip the ends into points. Snip the back ends but leave them loose.

Make and sew in a lining (see p. 130) and attach some elastic (see p. 126).

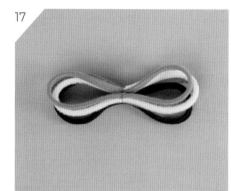

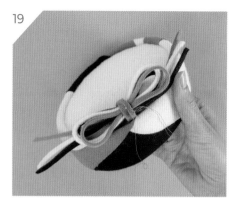

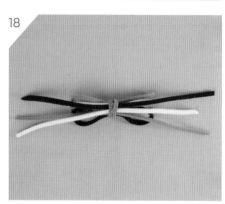

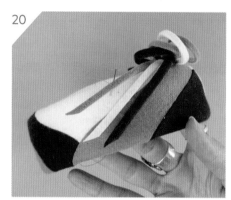

Why not try...
playing with the patchwork pattern;
experiment with how the felt is cut,
the quantity of pieces, colors, and
textures.

Upcycled Straw Hat

MATERIALS

- preowned straw hat
- no. 5 petersham ribbon—enough to fit inside the head fitting, and at least a few times around the outside of the crown
- no. 3 / no. 5 petersham ribbon—enough to cover the brim edge plus a little more. I have used no. 3; you may want to use the larger no. 5 if you are a beginner.
- bias strip of buckram—see step 14
- bias strips of sinamay—2 at 4" x 10" (10 x 25 cm) for the trim, and 1 at 19⅝" x 4" (50 x 10 cm) for the hatband
- matching thread
- lining fabric

EQUIPMENT

- sewing kit
- iron
- pressing cloth (organza/organdie)
- folded cloth or press pad
- kettle/steamer
- wire cutters / pliers
- pegs/clips
- curling tongs (optional)
- tailor's chalk

A take on the trilby; dress it up or down by playing with different trims.

Old hats can be given new life by refreshing their shape and trim. The level of redesign is up to you and will depend partly on the item. Old hat materials can often be great quality, so look out for them in charity shops, thrift stores, antiques markets, and vintage stores. This vintage paradisal sun hat has been transformed into a chunky trilby style.

Preparing the hat

1. Study the hat to decide where the CF and CB sit. If the hat has a head ribbon, the join of this and label should sit at the CB. Mark the CB and CF with a pin.

2. Carefully remove any trims, head ribbons, wires, stitches, and linings.

Removing dents and dirt

3. If there are dirty marks on the straw, some can be removed with a little steam, then brushing the area with a soft pile fabric; velvet is ideal for this. Placing some sticky tape over a mark and scratching the surface with a pin before removing again can also lift dirt.

If the hat is dented, warm each area in need of "repair" with an iron, focusing on one dent at a time. Take a folded cloth or press pad and hold inside the shape for support. Working on top, cover the surface with a pressing cloth to avoid scorching, and gently iron out and smooth over the dents. Some stubborn creases may require a short burst of steam before ironing. **(image a)**

Hold the area in shape, supporting the inside and outside with your fingertips until it cools. **(image b)** Alternatively, if you have a suitable crown block you would like to use, reblock on that and pull a string around the headline to secure. A block may be required if the hat body is very crumpled.

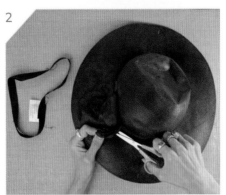

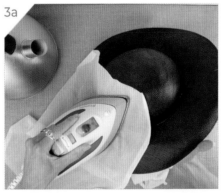

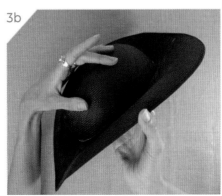

4. Gently iron the brim flat under a cloth on a flat surface, with a little steam from the iron or kettle.

Add extra stiffener now if required.

Shortening the brim

5. Decide how wide you would like the brim. Brims tend to be shorter at the back and widest at the front, differing by half an inch or so. Starting at the headline at the CB, measure and mark with chalk the depth of brim you would like. Do the same at the CF, then the sides. Make a mark every inch or so, making sure the measurements are symmetrical, then join the marks with a curved line. In this case the back is 1½" (4 cm), sides 2" (5 cm), and front 2⅓" (6 cm). The offcut can be kept for another trim.

Cut at this line. Move the CF and CB pins inward if necessary.

Shape a wire to fit the brim edge and sew on using wire stitch, making sure the join is at the CB (see p. 28).

Making the rolled petersham edge

6. Starting and ending at the CB, measure around the brim edge. Use the tape measure on its side so it curves accurately. Add 1⅕" (3 cm) to this measurement, then cut a length of petersham this size.

7. Bring the ends of the petersham together, pin them at ⅗" (1.5 cm) from the end, then sew with a backstitch and press open the seam.

8. Pin the petersham join to the CB, then pin around the entire shape, working in N–S, E–W positions until it holds securely.

5

6

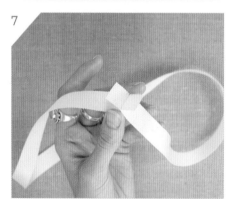

7

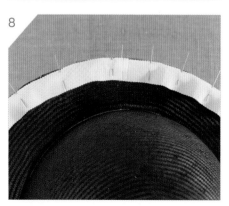

8

9. Starting at the CB, sew the petersham ⅕" (0.5 cm) in from the wired edge with a backstitch, with the long stitches on the petersham. Make each backstitch roughly ⅖" (1 cm); if they are too small it can weaken the straw. When you reach the CB, go over your first stitch, oversew, and tie off.

10. Roll the petersham over the edge and pin on the underside.

11. Stab-stitch through the scalloped edge of the petersham on the underside, then bring your needle through the straw, coming out just under the rolled edge on the other side, then stab-stitch back down under the rolled edge and through to the scalloped edge again.

Heightening the crown

This hat is very shallow, and in order to form the trilby-style dents in the top, it needs to be made taller.

12. Measure and note down the circumference of the headline.

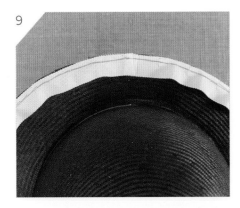

13. Add pins at the CB and CF on the crown. Measure up ⅘" (2 cm) from the headline all the way around the crown, and mark with chalk. Insert scissors into this line and cut the crown away.

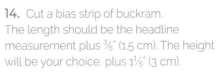
14. Cut a bias strip of buckram. The length should be the headline measurement plus ⅗" (1.5 cm). The height will be your choice, plus 1⅕" (3 cm).

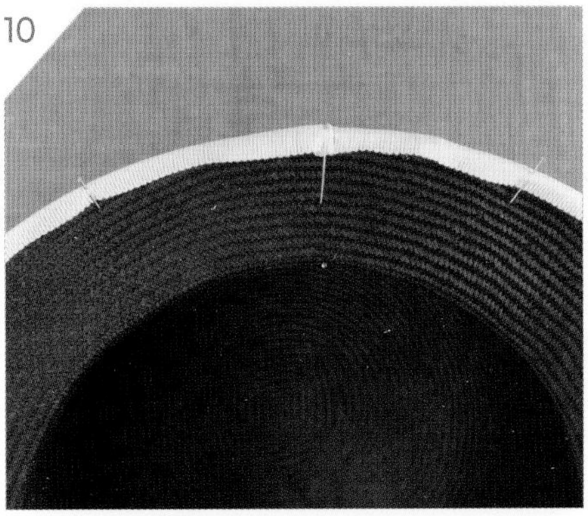

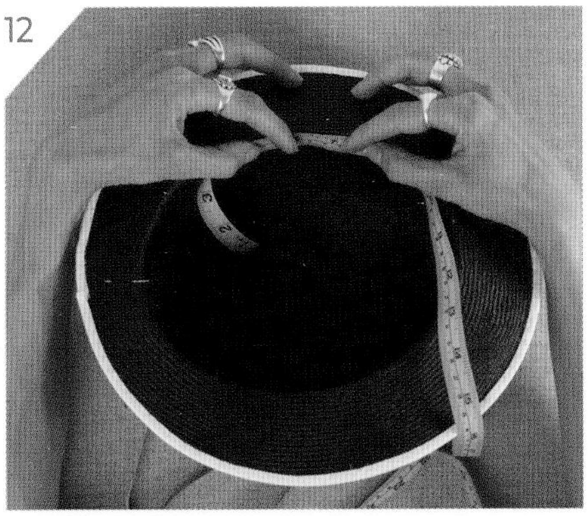

Overlap the ends together by ⅗" (1.5 cm), pin together, check it fits inside the headline, then sew the ends together with a diagonal stitch.

Insert the buckram inside the crown, match up the CB, and pin around in N–S, E–W positions, overlapping the edges by ⅗" (1.5 cm).

15. Sew together using a backstitch.

Sew in the petersham head ribbon to the brim headline now (see p. 30).

Joining the Crown and Brim
16. Bend the petersham back so you can access the headline, then place the crown inside the brim, overlapping the crown and brim by ⅗" (1.5 cm). Pin together and sew with a backstitch.

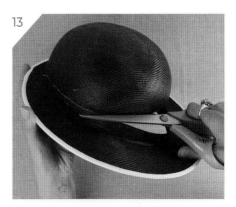

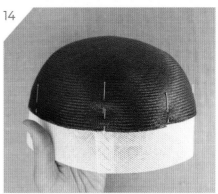

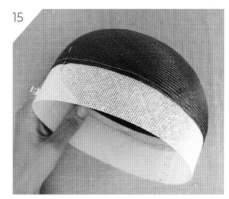

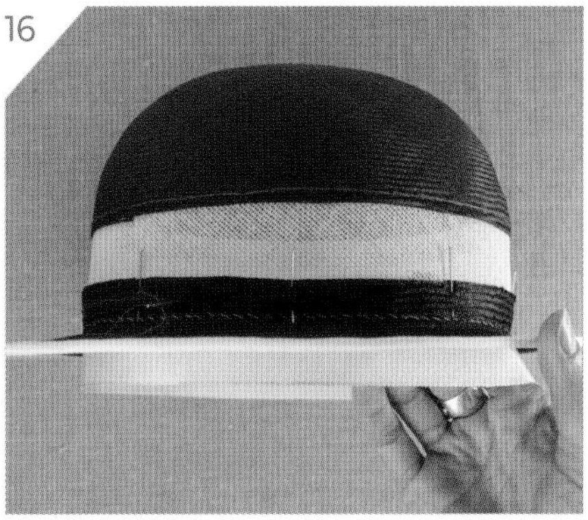

Reshaping the crown

17. To add a dent in the top of the crown, begin by lightly steaming the tip. Now, supporting the inside of the hat with one hand, use the side of your other hand to form a dent.

Refine the shape by heating with an iron through a cloth and shaping with your fingers, in the same way the original dents were removed.

18. Lightly steam the front of the tip and, with one hand underneath as before, pinch the front to create two even dents either side, making sure the point of the pinch is at the CF. Iron to neaten.

Assembling the hatband

19. Measure around the headline, then add 1²⁄₅" (3 cm) to this measurement. Cut two or three lengths of no. 5 petersham at this measurement—you'll need enough to cover the buckram join. Pin one to another along their length—this can be sewn with a small, neat backstitch, but more effectively on a sewing machine. If required, pin and sew the third strip to the others, and more if required. This is your hatband.

20. Cut another two lengths of petersham that will fold around the petersham hatband width, with ²⁄₅" (1 cm) overlap. Here I have used a navy-blue piece from the petersham I cut out of the original hat. Sew the two lengths together as above, then sew the ²⁄₅" (1 cm) overlap to form a loop. Slide the loop onto the hatband, with the join on the side intended for the inside.

Sew the ends of the hatband together at ³⁄₅" (1.5 cm) from the ends with a backstitch.

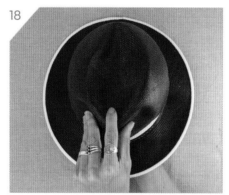

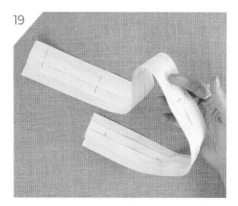

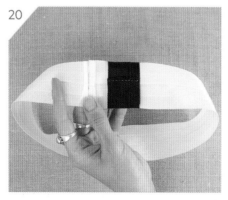

21. Take the two 4" x 10" (10 x 25 cm) bias-cut sinamay strips. Follow steps 18–26 on p. 42; however, stretch the sinamay by pulling it under a warm iron first, since this narrows the weave and creates a more dense-looking material.

Follow steps 18–20 only for the longer strip—the ends can stay raw.

22. Create tight spirals on the two shorter strips by curling around tongs, or around your fingers (with a little steam to soften it first).

23. Arrange the hatband over the crown, with the join sitting between the left side and CF. Pull the longer sinamay strip tightly around the band, with the ends matching the hatband join. Overlap the ends by ²⁄₅" (1 cm), then sew together. Slide over the petersham loop to cover the joins.

24. Arrange the spirals through the loop and tie-tack them in a few locations, tying off the threads on the inside of the hat. Do enough so they are fixed in position. Then tie-tack down the bow loop, as indicated by the pins in the image. Add another tie tack at the bottom of the hatband at the back, and on the opposite side.

Add a subtle curve to the brim by gently bending the wire downward at the front.

Last, add a lining to finish (see p. 130).

21
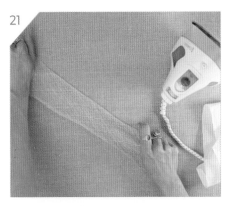

25

Why not try . . .
transforming an old felt hat; the
method works for that too.

22
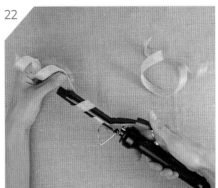

23

24

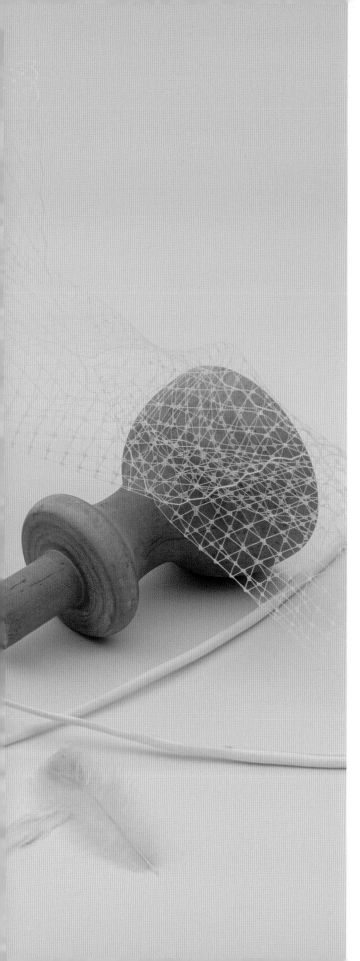

ADDITIONAL TRIMS
ALTERNATIVE WAYS TO DECORATE YOUR HATS

In this chapter we look at a range of traditional trims and techniques. They can be added to any hat or used on a small base or Alice band to form headpieces on their own.

Feathers

There are many options for using feathers in millinery, such as duck, goose, peacock, ostrich plumes, coq, large turkey broads, pheasant, hackle, and delicate guinea fowl. They are available in an array of colors, some with prints, or with etched or laser-cut patterns.

Here are some introductory techniques that can be used to transform a wide range of feathers, giving different effects on each type. For attachment methods, see Quills (p. 117).

Stripping

To create an elegant, neat trim, feathers can be partly stripped of their fronds to leave a long "stemlike" spine.

The fastest way to achieve this is by pulling the fronds down the spine from tip to base, beginning at the point you want your stem to start. (image 1)

Sometimes this technique can be a little clumsy on chunkier feathers and damage the remaining spine, so the fronds can also be trimmed off by cutting close to the spine with a scalpel.

On a cutting mat or protected surface, place the feather with the side to be cut on the side you hold your knife. Steadying the spine with the other hand, cut toward yourself, from tip to base. Cut slowly and gently, taking care with the blade. (image 2)

Whichever method you use, then rub with fine sandpaper or a nail file to remove any rough areas. (image 3)

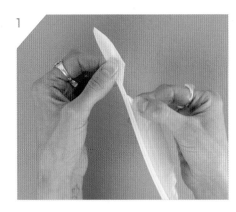

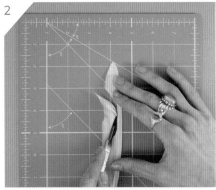

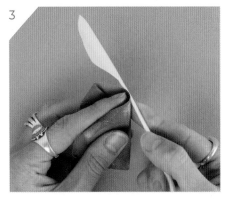

Cutting

To neaten or alter the natural outline of a feather, make sure the fronds are lying flat and not overlapping. Cut using a sharp pair of scissors, scalpel, or rotary cutter. Cut against the direction of the fronds, since this gives some tension to work against and the fronds don't slip as you cut. (image 4).

If you're struggling to get a clean line, try placing a strip of masking tape over the feather to stop the fronds from moving, then cut. Remove the tape once finished. You can also draw a pattern on to the tape to create more-adventurous shapes. (image 5)

Interesting patterns can be created by snipping into the feather. Feathers 1–3 have been cut by snipping into the fronds in a straight line toward the spine; feather 4, by stripping one side and then snipping the other at an angle; feather 5, by stripping high from the base, then snipping a shape into the top; and feather 6 by stripping sections and snipping off the tip. (image 6)

4

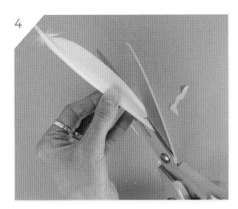

Curling

The fronds can be curled in multiple ways. They can be teased between your index finger and thumbnail (image 7), curled with scissors, using a lightness of touch as if curling a gift ribbon (image 8), and with heated curling tongs if the fronds are long enough.

The spines can also be curled, using the techniques detailed in the Quills section.

7

5

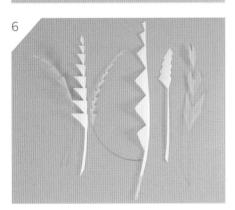

8

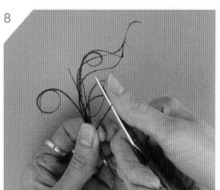

6

Feather mounts

Feather mounts are groups of feathers that have been refined using the methods above, then arranged like a bouquet and bound together, ready to sew to a hat. Here is a simple mount using three sets of the same groups of feathers, but you can try this with any number, style, size, and color of feathers you wish; just take into consideration how the colors, shapes, and textures work together. It can be a fiddly process at first, but, as always, practice makes it easier!

MATERIALS
- feathers (see step 1)
- thread
- extra-fine millinery wire 10" (25cm)

EQUIPMENT
- sewing kit
- superglue

1. Select your feathers. I have used three sets of the following:
5 strands of an ostrich plume
2 blush coq
1 black coq
1 hen church window
1 natural goose quill
2 silver hackle
1 neon-pink goose biot (optional. Only one required for the last stage)

2. Cut, strip, and curl your first set of feathers, and trim any long spines so they are a roughly ⁴⁄₅" (2 cm) longer than you would like for the mount. If they are chunky, snip the spines at an angle to avoid bulk.

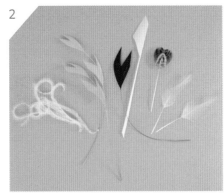

3. Place your glue in easy reach. Cut a length of thread roughly 19⅔" (50 cm), and a length of extra-fine millinery wire at approx. 2¾" (7 cm) for each set (other wires will work as long as they are fine and strong).

Holding the wire in one hand, bring the feathers around it, overlapping the top of the wire with the base of the spines by an inch or so, and arrange them as you wish. They can be tweaked later.

4. Once you are happy with their position, pick up the length of thread from the middle to create a U shape, and drape this over the area where the feathers and wire overlap. Pull the loose ends of the thread through the loop and pull tight.

5. Bind the cotton around the feathers and wire. The easiest way to do so is by pulling the thread around a few times, then twirling the mount while holding the thread taut. The thread will slip in one direction but grip in the other.

Once you have covered the spines, add a tiny dab of glue along the length of the bind, leave to dry, then snip off the excess thread. If you run out of thread, just start a new piece where you finished the first.

Prepare each set of feathers so you have three small mounts.

4

5

6. Bring together the three small mounts so they sit at the same height. The heights can be staggered to create a long, bushier mount if you are using a thicker bunch of feathers. Curl a neon-pink goose biot with tongs and add to the center, then bind everything together with thread at the bottom of the existing binds. Take this final bind to the end of the wires and go back on yourself a few turns before sewing the thread through the bind and knotting. A tiny dot of glue can be added for extra security. **(image 6a)**

Tweak and recurl the feathers if required.

Your mount is now ready to be sewn onto a hat. The bound wires can be bent into different positions to form a sturdy base that can be sewn on top of a hat, poked through and sewn to the underside, or sewn to an Alice band. **(image 6b)**

6a

6b

Tips

• If you would like to use natural untreated or "found" feathers, any germs or mites that may be on them can be killed by placing them in a sealed container in a freezer for a minimum of two weeks.

• Many feathers come in two different directions, leaning either left or right. Take this into consideration when designing and purchasing them.

• If your feathers are looking tired, waft them through some steam and gently run your fingers over the fronds to straighten them out.

This image shows some stripped and cut goose feathers on an Alice band with the Birdcage Veil project, which follows.

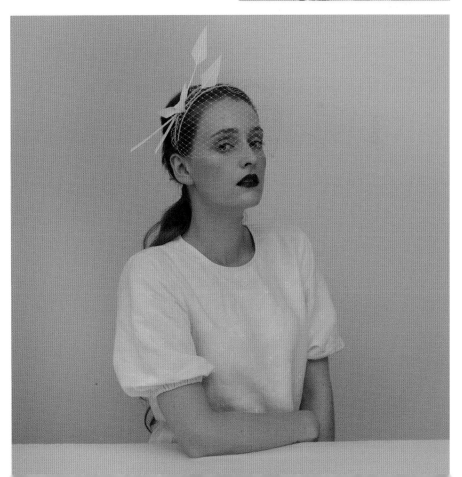

Birdcage Veil

MATERIALS
- 19⅔" x 7⅞" (50 x 20 cm) length of veiling
- 29½" (75 cm) strong millinery wire for the Alice band
- 2" x 35½" (5 x 90 cm) strip of tulle on the stretch for the Alice band
- matching thread

EQUIPMENT
- sewing kit
- marker pen
- iron

This birdcage veil is simple and versatile; it can be sewn to a hat base, or an Alice band as shown here. I have used veiling with holes approx. ⅗" (1.5 cm) in width, but larger versions are available. The style can be enlarged by increasing the length and depth of the veiling to your desired size.

1. Lay out the veiling and iron with steam to flatten.

Measure 5⁷⁄₁₀" (14.5 cm) up the left side of the veiling, to the top of the nearest little square, then, following the diagonal line of the veiling, measure across to the top (roughly 5½" (14 cm). Cut here, leaving the diagonal line of little squares intact.

2. Measure up 5⁷⁄₁₀" (14.5 cm) on the other side and cut the same. The length across the top should be roughly 6½" (16.5 cm), depending on the size of weave of veiling you have used (see image). Make a small tie tack in the center along the top.

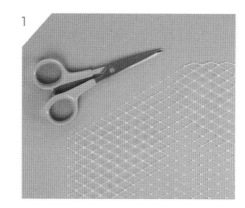

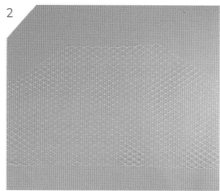

3. Cut a length of thread roughly 19⅔" (50 cm) and knot the end. Add a pen mark along the thread from the knot at roughly 11⅞" (30 cm). This will be your guide for the veiling when gathered.

4. Oversew a couple of times on the bottom square of the veiling. Now sew a running stitch through the squares of veiling, going up through one, down through the next, and so on (see image). Sew around the entire shape. You will probably need to start gathering the veiling a little in order to keep enough thread to reach the end.

5. Gather the veiling to the pen mark on the thread by pulling on the loose end of thread. Oversew on the last square just before the pen mark, to secure the gather.

6. The veil can now be positioned onto the base of your choice. To make the Alice band, see p. 127.

To fix the veiling to the Alice band, measure up 1⅓" (3.5 cm) from each end of the band and mark with a pin on the back wire (the side with the join).

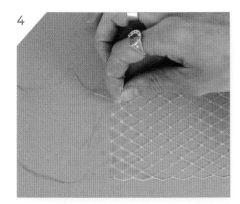

4

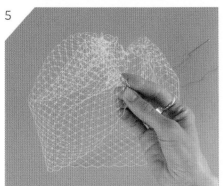

5

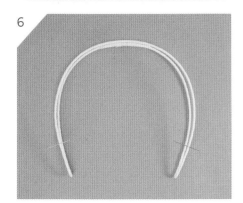

6

7. Pin the bottom corners of the veil at these points, making sure the veil falls over the front wire. Even out the gathers with your fingers, then pin the center of the veil to the CB of the Alice band (the center of the join). Now pin the midpoints, then the areas in between, readjusting the gathers as you go if required. Pin through the squares into the tulle of the Alice band.

8. Sew the veiling to the band by running small diagonal stitches through the tulle and each of the squares, making sure each end is fastened securely. Remove the pins as you go, so they don't get caught up in your stitches (see image).

The gathering stitches can now be removed and any untidy areas snipped away from the Alice band.

The veil can be tie-tacked to the front of the Alice band if you would like the shape to lie flatter. You can now sew your choice of trims or beading detail to the veil, or leave it simple.

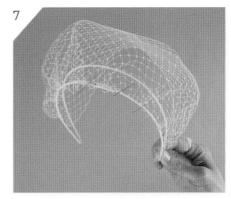

7

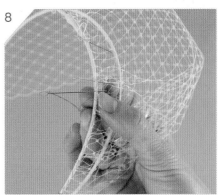

8

Why not try . . .
· adding some sparkle to the veiling by gluing on some craft crystals to the squares with a little dab of beading glue. Apply the glue neatly by using a pin to dot it on.

Quills

Quills (or spines) are the center part of a feather and make beautiful trims. The quills often used in millinery are ostrich feathers stripped of their fronds.

They can be used simply with their natural curve or shaped. The fine tip bends very easily. However, as you approach the thicker parts of the quill, they will require more work in order to shape, and the thickest area at the base is more brittle and may not bend at all. Bear in mind the natural line of the quill as you mold them, since trying to bend against its curve may cause it to crease or split.

Curling with a wand / hair tongs

Once your tongs are hot, hold the thin end of the quill at an angle, placing it at the base under the clasp, or in your hand on the handle of the curling wand. Slowly pull the quill around the wand, easing it around in small sections as it softens under the heat. (image 1)

As the quill thickens, it will need to be pulled tighter and rocked back and forth slowly to ease it around without creasing.

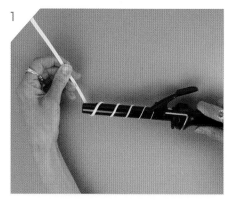

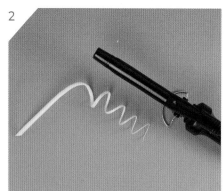

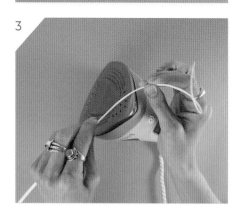

Once shaped, lift from the wand and let cool. (image 2)

You can also hold the tongs between your knees and press the soft side of the quill against the tongs in the same way as with the iron (see below).

Over an iron

The edge of an iron can be used to manipulate a quill in a controlled manner, if you require a particular shape rather than an even spiral. Press the quill over the iron edge, then, working on an inch or so, move it back and forth until it starts to soften and mold under the light pressure. This tends to work well for the thicker part of the quill. (image 3)

Steaming/soaking and setting around tubular shapes

Quills can be softened very effectively by letting them soak for ten to fifteen minutes in boiling water. You will need a heatproof tray or fish kettle to lay them in (image 4) Alternatively, you can hold them in steam until they become malleable. Once softened, they can be pulled around many objects to achieve interesting curls, twirls, and angles.

Try easing quills around a broom handle or cardboard tubes of differing widths, securing them down with string, tape, or elastic until dry. (image 5)

Curling with scissors

Quills can be manipulated by pulling them over the blunt edge of scissor blades or a pencil, in the same way as a gift ribbon. Press the soft underside of the quill over the blunt edge of the scissors gently, repeating the action to build a curve. Angle the scissors so it starts to form a twist rather than curling straight over itself. Start at the top and work down, curving an inch at a time. This method is more suited to subtle curves. (image 6)

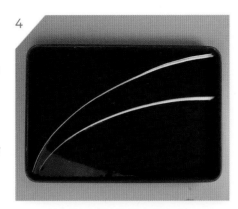

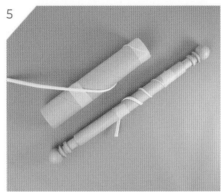

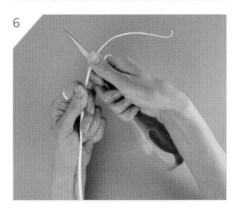

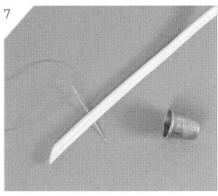

Straightening

The curve of a quill can be removed by placing it under a pressing cloth and steam-ironing it. You'll need to hold the base in one hand and iron in the other in order to control the shape. After steam-ironing it for a few moments, hold it tight until it sets the shape.

Finishing ends

The ends of quills tend to look better when cut at an angle. This can easily be done with a strong pair of paper or buckram scissors or a scalpel, cutting away from the spine, into the direction of the end. Smooth the cut surface of the end with fine sandpaper. Sandpaper can also be used to remove any rough fibers from the length of the spine, although this should be done before shaping.

Attaching quills

The most secure way to attach a quill is also the most attractive and least damaging. Push your needle sideways through the soft part of the quill, not from back to front, since this will prevent it splitting down the hard front surface. (image 7)

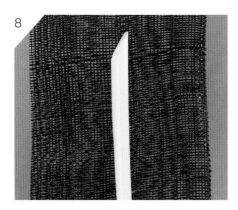

8

9

Using a double thread, sew at least twice through this point to the base, before securing on the underside of the base with a knot. Repeat in another location on the spine to minimize movement. **(images 8 and 9)**

If your quill is difficult to sew through, try heating your needle over a flame before pushing through the quill.

Coloring

Quills can be purchased in many shades. They can be colored easily with spray paints, acrylic paints, even nail polish, which, although time consuming, gives an opulent enamel finish. When painting, it helps to work on half the quill, then let it dry before working on the other half. That way you can hold the dry part and rest it on this section while the other half dries. I use pegs to hang or prop the quill (see p. 70 of the Hand-Shaped Felt Saucer project).

Why not try . . .
• experimenting by shaping quills around items containing angles, such as table legs.

This image shows curled quills on an Alice band with the Versatile Rose project, which follows.

Versatile Rose

MATERIALS

- cotton organdie—enough to cut at least 12 petals, 2 large and 2 small leaves, one calyx, 1 bud, and a 4⅓" x 1½" (11 x 4 cm) rectangle—approx. 13¾" x 11⅘" (35 x 30 cm) in total; silk or silk organza can also be used
- two 4¾" (12 cm) and one 3" (8 cm) lengths of fine millinery wire (Strong beading wire and fabric flower making wire can also be used. This rose can also be made without a wire, sewing the petals to the bud only, which can be sewn straight to a hat.)
- matching thread

EQUIPMENT

- sewing kit
- flower patterns (see p. 152)
- bradawl or blunt knife
- wire cutters / pliers
- iron
- stiffener
- fabric glue

Flowers are an eternally popular trim for millinery; however, flower making is an art in itself, with entire books and specialist equipment dedicated to it. Using only the basic sewing kit, we shall make a classic flower that, with a few adaptations, can form an array of different finishes (see p. 62 for an adaptation in felt).

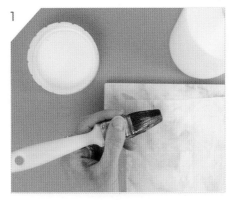

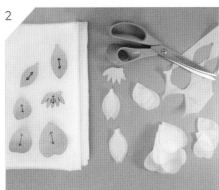

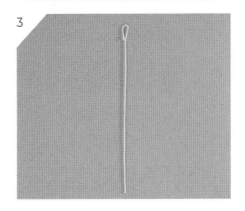

Preparing the organdie

1. Iron the organdie, then paint with stiffener. I have used water based (see image). This can be hung to dry, but I prefer to use a hairdryer on a low power setting. This speeds up the process and avoids the stiffener draining down the fabric, which can happen when left to dry naturally. I lay the hairdryer on a table so both hands can control the material.

2. Once your fabric is dry, draw on and cut three small, four medium, and five large petals; one calyx; and two large and two small leaves in organdie. Cut one large and one small leaf in adhesive webbing.

Creating the bud

3. Take one 4¾" (12 cm) length of wire and bend over the tip to make a small loop.

4. Cut a bias rectangle 4⅓" x 1½" (11 x 4 cm). Fold the long edges into the center, then fold in half lengthways.

5. Tie a loose knot in the middle of the folded strip, then wrap the ends around the wire loop, with the point of the knot facing up. Pin to secure.

6. Stitch through the ends of the fabric near the knot, bind it around the ends a few times, then tie off to secure. This acts as the bud and forms a secure base on which to sew petals.

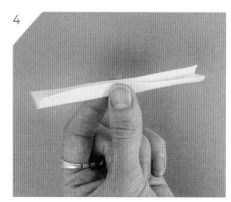

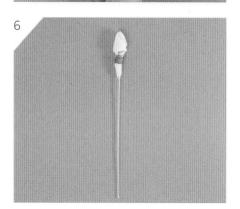

Shaping the petals

7. Roll the top edges of each petal so they curve over by pushing the edge gently between your fingers and thumbs.

Cup the petals by folding two pleats at each base, then stretch a deeper curve into them by pushing out across the bias with your thumbs and fingertips in the center of the petal.

Constructing the flower

8. Note: The same length of thread can be used to sew on multiple petals before securing and tying off. Fold one of the small petals around the bud, with the top of the petal placed slightly higher than the top of the bud, then sew together with a couple of stitches across the petal overlap.

9. Place the next small petal with its center opposite the center of the first, and sew with a couple of stitches.

7

10. Add the petals one by one, in size order. Secure each with a couple of stitches at the base, taking the needle through one or two layers of petals. Every few petals, raise the height of the tops of the petals very slightly. Work around in a spiral, spacing them so they overlap by half a petal each time (the edge of the new petal starts on top of the center of the previous). After the last petal, tie off the thread to secure. **(images 10a, b, and c)**

10a

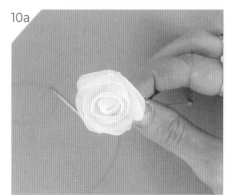

8

10b

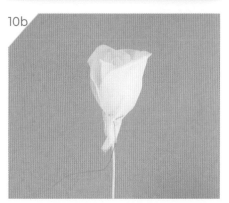

9

10c

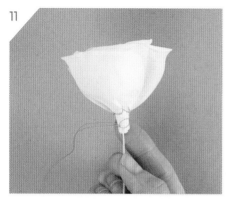

11. Cut roughly 31½" (80 cm) of thread, fold in half, then bring around the base of the flower. Pull the loose ends through the loop that the folded thread creates.

12. Bind the thread around the base a few times, then neatly down the stem to around halfway. Add a dot of glue to secure.

13. Fold around the calyx so it sits snugly around the base, add a couple of tiny dots of glue to secure it to the base of the petals, and then tie-tack the edges of the calyx together, catching the petal beneath. I have colored the calyx with green ink here so it can be seen more clearly.

Creating the leaves

14. Take one of the larger organdie leaf shapes and place the adhesive webbing over the top, then place the end of the second 4¾" (12 cm) length of wire in the center of the leaf, stopping just before the leaf tip.

15. Place the second organdie leaf over the top and iron through a cloth until they fuse together.

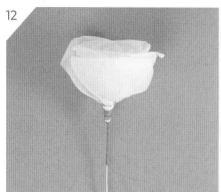

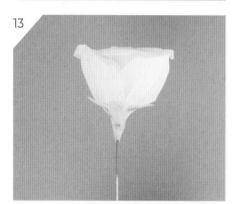

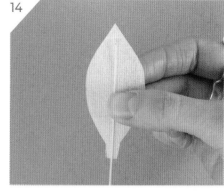

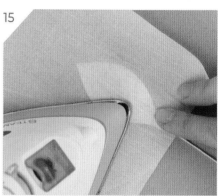

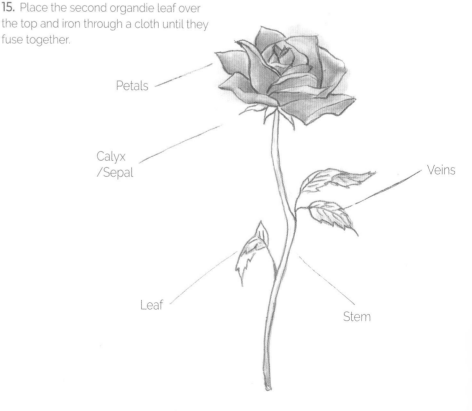

Petals

Calyx /Sepal

Veins

Leaf

Stem

16. Place the leaf on a soft surface such as an ironing board or folded fabric. Score veins into the petals by heating the tip of a bradawl or a blunt knife with an iron, then running it from the wired center out toward the edge.

17. Snip little triangles into the edges at an angle, to form a natural-looking silhouette.

Repeat steps 14–17 for the smaller leaf.

18. Fold the tabs at the base of the leaves around the wire, then bind halfway down each wire in the same way as the rose.

Place the leaf stems together. Bend the smaller wire ²⁄₅" (1 cm) down from the leaf, then bind together from this point down, to roughly halfway along the wires. Make sure the new bind covers the end of the first bound wires.

19. Now place the rose with the leaves, and bind a thread down the length of the wires to the bottom. Secure the thread with a small stitch, then a little dot of glue to finish.

Manipulate the wire into an attractive shape. The flower is now ready to sew onto your chosen hat. It can be left as a stem or bent around and hidden under the flower.

Tips
• This flower can look very different by altering the size, shape, number, or fabric of the petals. For example, using fewer petals will create a younger "rosebud" look. Or just using four or five petals that have been given fewer curves in the shaping process will result in a flower reminiscent of a pansy. The felt flower on p. 62 has been made using only a few of the petals.
• Color can be added to the petals with fabric dye, watercolor, and ink pens. Diluting the colors and building them up in layers can give a soft natural look.

Why not try . . .
• taking apart a real flower to copy the shape of its petals.
• bonding together different types of materials such as sinamay and organza to create unusual textures.

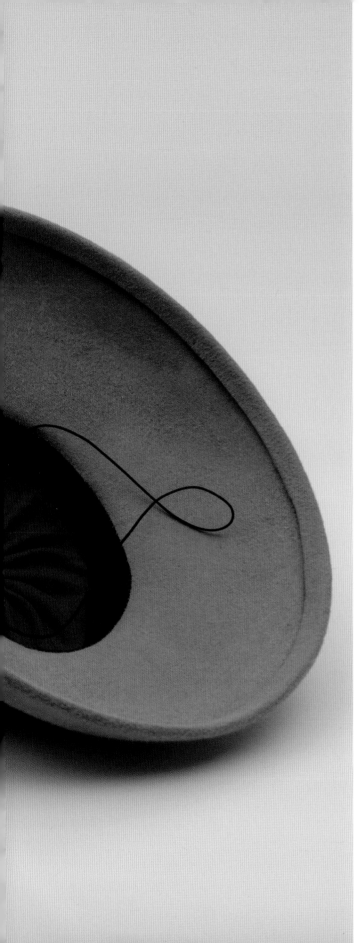

FINISHING TOUCHES
ADDING THE FINAL DETAILS

The way a hat is finished has a huge impact on its overall appearance, where a comparatively small effort can greatly improve its quality.

Comfort and ease of wear also rely on these final steps. The choice of lining, placement on the head, and shape and security of the attachment are vital in making a hat wearable, so it's always worth taking a little time to get it right.

Attaching Hats to Heads

The most-common ways to keep hats on are with elastic or an Alice band. Adding a comb is great for additional support.

Elastic

Usually used on smaller headpieces.

1. Use a good-quality, round elastic, approx. 1–2 mm diameter. The elastic should be cut long enough to go from the edge of the hat, under the hairline, and back up to the other edge of the hat. It needs to be tight enough not to slip, but not too tight. It can be pulled tighter if required.

Elastics can be colored with good-quality, flat-tipped marker pens (these give the most-even coverage); the elastics can be matched to hair colors prior to fixing to the hat (see image). They can also be dyed.

2. As a general rule, the elastic should be positioned at the halfway point between CB and CF on the base, but always try it on by pinning the elastic in place before sewing.

To fix it to the hat, push the end of the elastic between the stitches of the petersham and the edge of the hat. You can bend the tips of a hairpin / bobby pin flat and use it as a guide to pull through if required (see image). Double-knot the end of the elastic under the petersham.

3. Do the same on the other side. Check the fit on your head, then sew over the elastic just in front of the knot, going through the fabric of the hat. Be careful not to sew through the elastic, so that you can adjust the length if needed. Oversew three times and knot your thread to secure.

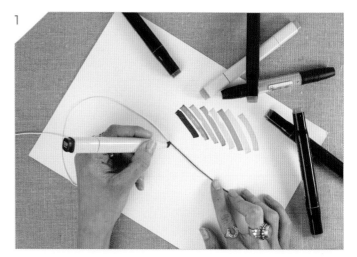

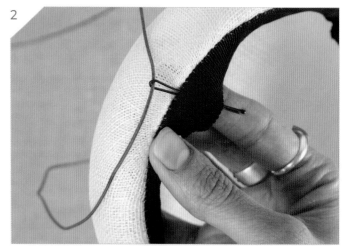

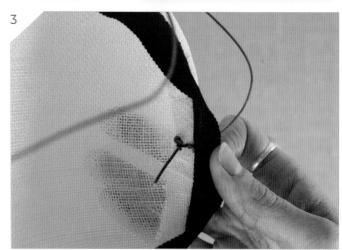

Alice bands and combs

These are great for hats that need to be worn in a specific way, since they are fixed into position. They can be stronger too if your hat is quite large. The tulle can be purchased or dyed in a shade to match either the hat or a specific hair color.

MATERIALS
- tulle approx. 2" x 35½" (5 x 90 cm), cut so it stretches along the length
- 29⅓" (74.5 cm) strong millinery wire
- metal comb

EQUIPMENT
- sewing kit
- pencil

1. To make a wire Alice band, cut a length of wire at 29⅓" (74.5 cm). Shape it into a flat circle with a 2" (5 cm) overlap. There is no need to take out the spring. Join the overlap (see p. 28).

2. Mark the center of the join with a pencil or pen. This is the CB.

3. Pulling the tape measure around the outer edge of the curve, measure 6$\frac{7}{10}$" (17 cm) down each side from the CB. Draw a mark, then bend at both points over your thumbnails to make a sharp angle. Make sure both bends go the same way.

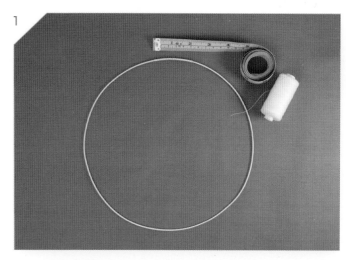

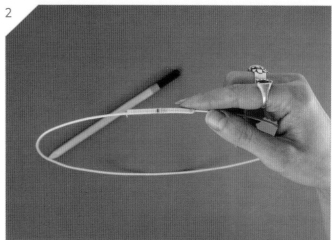

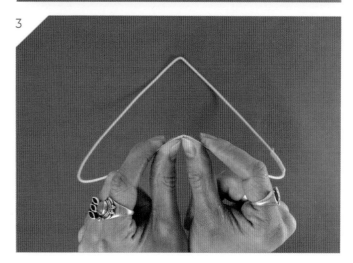

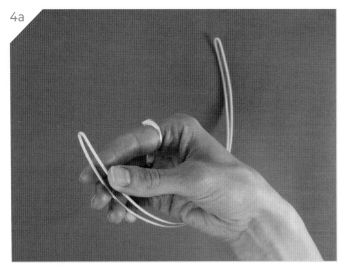

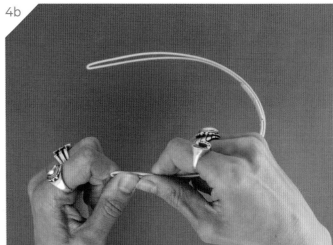

4. Squeeze the points to create a tighter angle. **(image a)** Give a slight outward bend to the ends, so they don't dig into the head. **(image b)** Open them up again so you have around 1⅕" (3 cm) in between the front and back. The back section should be slightly shorter than the front section. This is so the Alice band can sit on the head at a secure angle.

Bend the curve with gentle movements until it sits comfortably on the head.

5. Begin folding the end of the tulle in half along the length between your fingers, staggering the raw edges so they don't create a ridge.

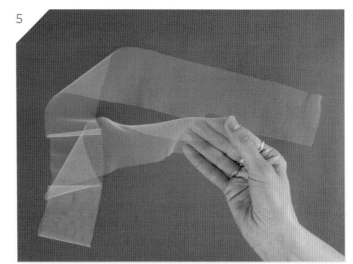

6. Starting at the CB of the wire, hold the end of the tulle on the wire with your thumb and begin winding the tulle tightly along the Alice band. The folded edge should sit closest to the CB, so that as you wind the tulle around, the raw edges are enclosed and the folded edge is on top (see image).

Keep winding the tulle around the wire, overlapping every ⅕" (0.5 cm) or so and keeping it at a sharp angle. Try to keep the tulle folded neatly as you go, since it is easy for it to twist on itself. The tulle will stay in place as you work down the wire. Keep binding, pulling carefully over the bent points, until you reach the CB again.

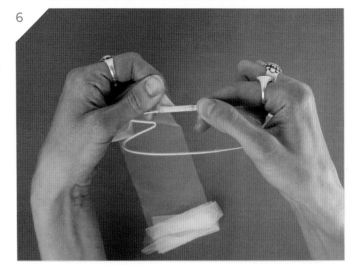

7. Pull the remaining tulle tightly over the CB, pin to secure it, then sew down, using tiny stitches. Trim the end of the tulle and neaten up any loose fibers so the join is nearly invisible.

8. If attaching to a hat, first decide the position by trying it on with the hat in the mirror, or on a mannequin, and pin in place. Sew it to the hat in three or four locations. Two on each side of the Alice band is best. Sew through the tulle to the hat, making sure the stitches can't be seen when the hat is worn.

Attaching the comb

9. Choose the most-discreet combs you can find. I find that small, flat, metal combs that can be bent to the shape of the head are best.

Position the comb so its prongs face toward the forehead. This is so the hat doesn't slide down over the face if the wearer bends forward. The comb is generally sewn at the back or side of the hat base or onto an Alice band. Use a double thread and sew around each prong at the base, catching the edge of the hat or the tulle of the Alice band. Be sure to fix the thread securely so it doesn't work loose.

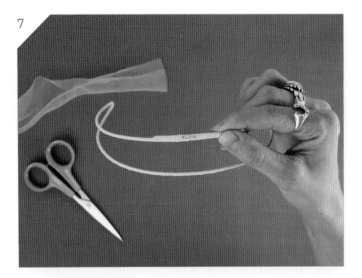

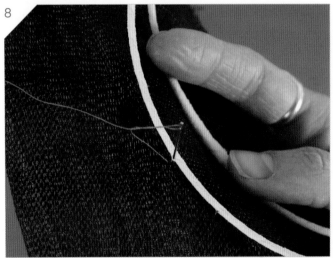

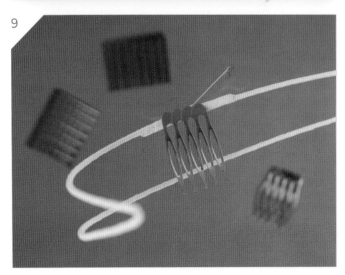

Linings

MATERIALS
- lining fabric (see steps 1–3)
- thread

EQUIPMENT
- sewing kit
- iron
- block or finished hat

Not all hats need linings, but sometimes adding a lining covers any construction work or rough areas on the inside and gives a high-quality finish.

This lining is very versatile and easy to make and can be altered to fit any size or depth of hat.

Choose an appropriate fabric for your hat. Look for something with enough structure to sit neatly inside the hat without flopping down, but not too thick and bulky.

1. Measure the inner circumference of the hat, taking the tape measure from the CB around the petersham and back to the CB.

2. Now measure the radius—from the petersham edge to the center of the hat. If the hat is oval, measure the longest part.

3. Add 1⅕" (3 cm) to each of these measurements.

Using these measurements, cut a rectangle of fabric on the bias. Fold in half with the right sides together, so the ends meet. Pin these ends, then sew ⅗" (1.5 cm) from the edge, using a backstitch. You can also use a sewing machine for this.

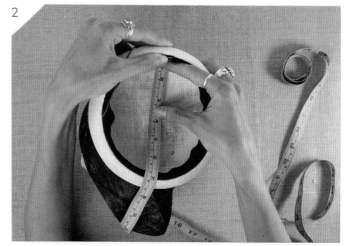

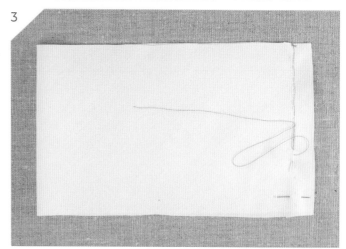

4. You'll now have a tube. Fold over one edge of the tube by ³⁄₅" (1.5cm)—fold it on the same side as the seam you have just sewn. Press the fold with your fingers to form a guide, then iron with the tip of an iron to form a strong crease. This edge will be the top.

5. Knot your thread, then starting at the CB, sew a running stitch approx. ¹⁄₅" (0.5cm) from the folded top, with a stitch length ²⁄₅" (1cm) wide along the folded edge. Gently pull the thread to gather up the fabric, creating a circle. Knot the ends of the thread a few times to secure and cut off the extra thread.

6. Cut a small circle of matching fabric, position over the hole and sew down with a small running stitch.

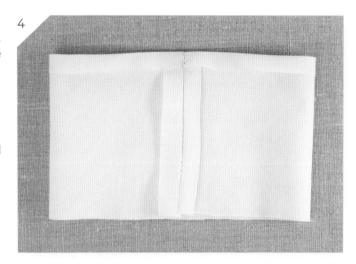

7. Lift up the petersham. Fit the lining inside the hat so the center gather sits in the middle, and match up the seam of the lining with that of the petersham at the CB. Fold back and hide the raw edges of the lining, making sure the edge of the lining sits just under the petersham, and it fits well around the shape.

Pin in place, then sew using a diagonal running stitch, catching the edge of the hat, just under the petersham, as you go.

8. Fold back the petersham head ribbon. This is now ready to be set.

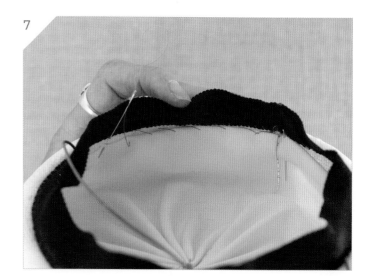

Setting the Head Ribbon

EQUIPMENT

- small, clean paintbrush and bowl of hot water
- tissue paper

A petersham head ribbon can be "set," to give a neat and smooth finish inside a hat.

1. For a petersham that has already been attached, paint it with a small brush and very hot water.

2. Stuff the hat tightly with tissue paper and let it dry.

3. Remove the paper; the petersham will have set neatly around the shape.

Tips

- Sometimes the headline requiring petersham is very curved. In order to fit the ribbon neatly into such a shape without wrinkles or puckers, it actually needs to be curved before attaching. Do this by forming a slight curve in the ribbon with your fingers on an ironing board, then steam-iron or iron under a pressing cloth or damp cloth (see image). The iron can leave shiny marks on the ribbon, so make sure the ironed side is used as the underside when sewing into the hat.

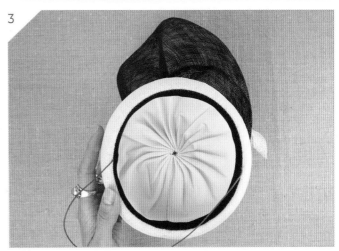

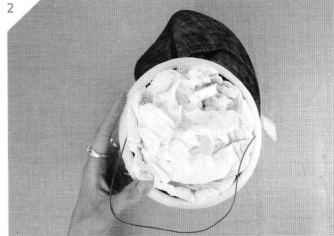

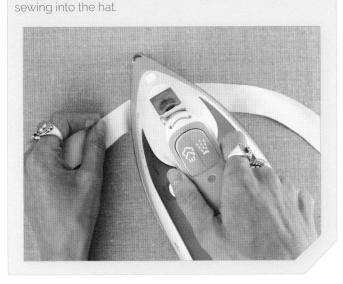

EXPANDING YOUR NEW SKILLS

DESIGN ADVICE AND EXERCISES

Finishing the projects in this book may represent just the beginning of your millinery journey. I hope they act as a springboard from which you can find your own ways of using what you've learned.

This chapter is designed to help you take your millinery skills further, encouraging the exploration of your own ideas through research, sketching, and experimentation, so you can continue to create designs that interest you.

Taking It to the Next Level

Whether you want to learn millinery simply for the pleasure of making or to begin creating your own ideas, it's worth embracing design. Design skills are especially important when it comes to creating your own unique pieces, and having a clear aesthetic is vital if you have ambitions to sell your work.

I have met many beginners who have questioned why the design process is necessary. When you have an idea already, why go back to the drawing board? The reason is, although that initial idea may be great, spontaneous ideas can soon fizzle out if you don't refuel the fire. Sometimes you really do have to get that hat out of your system, but so often if you free up your thoughts and experiment,

you'll find that "perfect" initial idea can be improved and even expanded into multiple new ones. You may abandon it altogether once you start to explore. It helps keep things interesting, and keep you interested. It's easy to skim over the *Define* and *Develop* steps of the design process outlined here, but they are what will keep your ideas flowing.

Here is a brief description of the design process:

Discover: Find your *inspiration*.

Define: *Research* and *explore* your inspiration.

Develop: *Generate ideas* and *experiment* through sketching and playing with shapes and materials.

Deliver: Refine ideas into workable hats and bring them to life.

Finding inspiration and designing is a complex and personal thing, and developing an approach that suits you takes time. Try to be patient with your own thought processes, go with the flow, and try not to overthink when recording ideas; they can be explored in depth later.

The purpose of this process is to try things out, experiment, then edit and refine until you're happy. Sometimes getting it "wrong" helps ideas develop. However, if it doesn't feel natural, try a change of direction, such as bringing in a new element or even removing one.

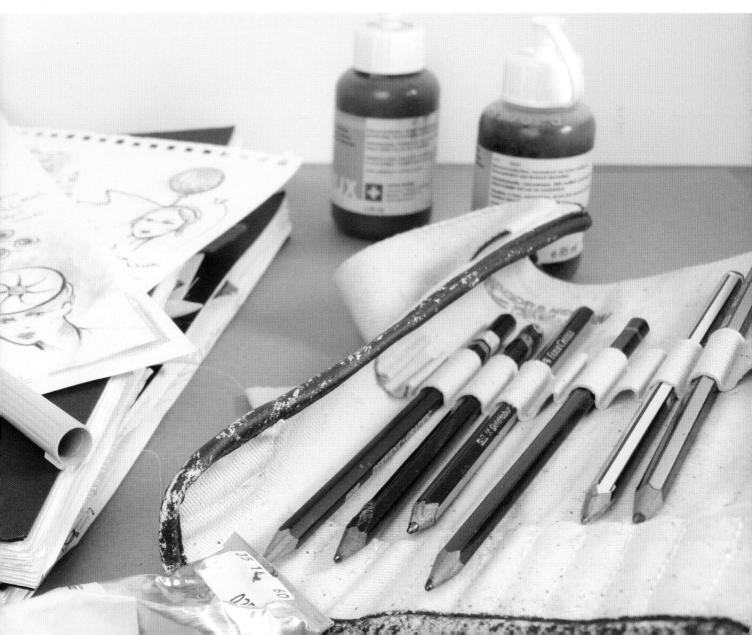

Inspiration, Themes, and Research

Inspiration

Inspiration is the key to creativity. However, finding your inspiration, or theme, can sometimes be tricky.

Your ideas are born through your choice of inspiration, and if you are intending to create more than one hat, it will also be from where you form a coherent look.

Your inspiration can be anything as long as it excites you and will give you enough ideas for your project. But don't panic about choosing it. If you get stuck, try something else.

For a couple of hats, it could be something as simple as a favorite vase; what are its form, colors, patterns, textures, origin, and scale? How can they be combined in a different order and placed on the head? You could even simply be led by your blocks and materials.

If you are thinking about putting together a range of hats, you may want to consider a wider inspiration source. Perhaps starting with a place, poem, painting, or historical era. Where can that painting take me? How can I bring the imagery of that poem together? How can I modify those historical styles?

Many modern ideas come from the past, since ideas go through cycles and eventually the old once again seems fresh. There are indeed some hat designs from the mid-twentieth century that could be mistaken as radically modern. However, when it comes to referencing existing design, new or old, it's a good idea to identify the detail you love and why, then find ways to personalize them.

Combining different ideas to form a coherent theme can be useful too. What if you mixed that historical hat detail with your favorite vase? Your designs may look quite different from the original source once they're developed.

Research your inspiration by gathering imagery

Inspiration imagery is generally broken down into two areas.

primary—The imagery is seen and recorded firsthand by you; for example, your own photos and sketches of a place.

secondary—The imagery is gathered from existing sources, such as paintings and objects depicting that place.

Knowing which visuals to leave out is as important as knowing what to include. In order to avoid getting confused or overwhelmed, gathering your imagery and editing out the bits that don't "fit" can help you understand the visual story you want your hat collection to tell. Laying out your images in mood boards, in sketchbooks, or just on a table is a great way to do this.

Inspiration theme generator exercise

Struggling to find that inspiration?

· Write down thirty or so words.

· Mix them up and randomly pull out two or three.

· Rearrange or repick them until they make sense to you.

· You could include everyday objects, places, activities, weather, moods or anything else.

You may surprise yourself with where they take you!

Here are a few to get you started:

stormy, plants, *sharp*, STRUCTURE, **creature**, soft, wall, l o o s e, **INDUSTRIAL**, play, **DRAMA**, dream, **rocks**, bird, **night**, hot, *day*, **machines**, house, pathway, **frozen**, pottery, *flowing*, shining, mirror, earth, **BLOCKS**, woven, abstract, *candy*, flying, softness, floral, ***water***, city, insect, **country**, beach, PATTERN.

This hat, from my *New Natural* collection, was inspired by the juxtaposition of natural fibers and plants with modern materials, where rough and smooth textures intertwine. Many ideas were tried to find the right balance through color, shape, texture, scale, and detail. The crown of the hat is blocked, while the trim and brim are made from flat patterns.

Drawing Heads and Hats

Sketching is a vital design tool; it helps us analyze and make sense of our ideas so we can begin to develop them and interpret them into real-world designs. But a lack of confidence can put people off.

If you're in need of help, try the following steps for drawing heads and hats at different angles, which will give you a base on which to build your design sketches.

Build each step on a single face and use a pencil so you can erase markings as you go. Some steps can be left out as you become familiar with the process—for example, the initial circle, or some facial features. You don't need to be an excellent illustrator; you can get your ideas across sufficiently by drawing the first few steps only—what is effectively an upside-down egg with a cross through the middle. But as always, the best way to improve is practice.

Front Angle

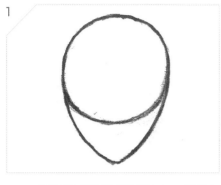

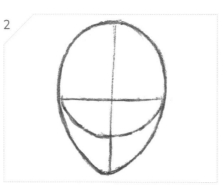

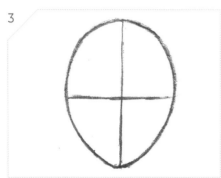

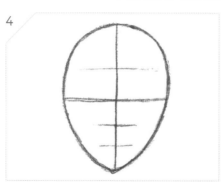

1. Draw a circle, then two curved lines that join in a point at the bottom.

2. Draw a cross though the center of the whole shape.

3. Erase the bottom of the circle.

4. Draw a short line centered between the top of the head and the middle line, then two lines in the bottom half, thus dividing this section into thirds. This gives you the right proportions for drawing in features.

5. Draw eyes positioned centrally on the middle line, a curve or nostril on the next line down, and lips on the lower line. Draw two vertical lines to represent the neck.

6. The top line represents the headline, and where a full hat would sit. When drawing on the hat, remember it usually sits lower at the back.

7. Erase the guide lines and add detail to your hat.

8. This image shows the same method with a small hat and hair added.

Three-Quarter Angle

1
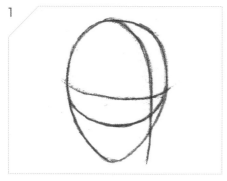

2
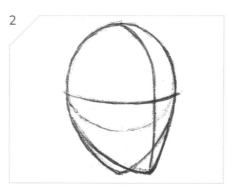

3
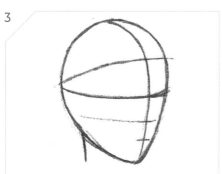

4

5

6
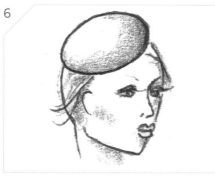

1. Draw a circle, then two curved lines that join in a point at the bottom to form the initial chin. Draw a curved line across the midway point between top and bottom. Starting at the center of the top of the shape, draw a line following the curve of the "forehead," then straight down to the bottom.

2. Change the position of the "chin" point so it sits to the right, at the bottom of the vertical straight line.

3. Erase the bottom of the circle and the initial chin point. Draw a horizontal curved line from the midway point on the right-hand side of the "forehead," bringing it down to meet the middle guide line at the back. Draw two small lines in the bottom half, which divide the section into thirds.

4. Draw features by using the vertical line as a guide; eyes at the midway line, nose on the line below, and lips on the bottom line. The top line will be where a full hat sits. The front sits above the eyes on the hairline, and the back just below the ears.

5. Erase the guide lines and add detail to the hat.

6. This image shows the same method but with the perching hat, hair, and some pencil shading.

Side Angle

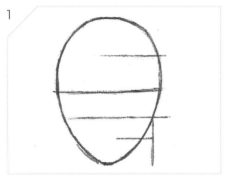
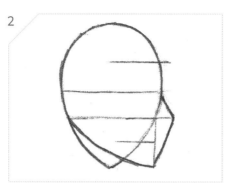
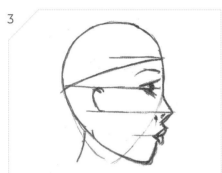
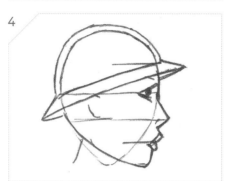

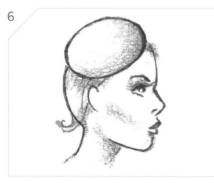

1. Draw the basic head shape as detailed previously. Draw a horizontal line across the midway point, then a line at the halfway point in the top section. Now draw two lines in the bottom half, dividing the section into thirds. Draw a vertical line, bringing it from the third line down to the same level as the bottom of the initial chin line.

2. Draw a new curve from the left side of the third line down, ending it at the bottom of the vertical line. Now draw a slight curve from the second line down out to the third line down, then from here to the bottom of the vertical line to create the new chin.

3. Draw the features, using the corresponding lines as guides. Draw a line from the right-hand side of the top line, down to the left side of the midline.

4. Draw the hat shape around the outside, using the line drawn in the previous step as a guide for placing the headline of the hat.

5. Erase the markings and add detail to the hat.

6. This image shows the same method but with the perching hat, hair, and shading.

Tips
• If you find this part challenging, you could draw many heads at once so they are ready for jotting down those lightbulb moments later.

Developing Designs

Beautiful things don't just look good by chance. Every detail has to be considered through design, and when it comes to translating your inspiration into hats, the way you do so will be unique. That may be through sketching, collaging, photographing shapes on a mannequin, or something else. Collecting and recording visual research, materials, and ideas in sketchbooks and mood boards helps form a coherent story, a place where you can translate your research into designs that can then be further explored and developed into 3-D toiles. They're also a great way to explain ideas to others.

Once you've gotten to grips with the core millinery materials, others can be fun to incorporate. Materials such as wood, paper, plastics, and metals all have complemented millinery well, as have additional techniques such as laser cutting. Part of the joy of millinery is its freedom when it comes to materials.

There are so many nuances to one's design process, but some things should be observed always. Below are some practicalities to consider.

Balance, line, and symmetry
It is a millinery tradition to use trims and shapes in odd numbers or to arrange things asymmetrically, which is usually more flattering. It's harder to get even numbers to work well visually, and sets of two can sometimes end up looking a bit like ears. However, symmetry has its place, and can achieve a stronger and often-fun look.

Symmetry/asymmetry should also be considered in the overall silhouette of your design, and where you want to draw the eye. Do you want to create an angled line with everything sweeping in one direction, or a centered look? In terms of balance, consider if it looks overly busy, too heavy, or too empty in some areas; if there is something to counteract this on the other side, or whether that is something you want to accentuate.

Shape and negative space
Take note of the shapes your elements are creating and how this affects the silhouette. Does the space in between the elements of the hat look good? Negative space can be as important as what is happening on the surface; it can give a sense of movement, lightness, or density.

Harmony
Do all the elements complement each other and work as a whole? This could be in terms of texture and color palette as well as shape and trims. Is there anything that can be left out? Don't overdo it!

Repetition
Multiples or groups of design elements, details, or trims can be used regularly or irregularly with great effect. Repetition can create unity, texture, and interest and add cohesiveness throughout a collection of hats.

Scale, dominance, and emphasis
Differing heights and sizes can help give interest; a dominant trim, base shape, texture, or color will attract the eye and draw attention to a focal point, and focal points can help a hat look complete. Are the trims subtle details or the main feature? What is the scale of the overall piece? Will this invite or deflect attention from the wearer and their outfit? You could think about how to emphasize the wearer's features, or how to draw attention to a certain element of a hat. A collection of hats can often benefit from a variation of scales.

Texture
Consider how the combination of materials affects the design. Are you aiming for a harder look with shiny materials and leather, or something softer with light, natural fabrics? Does it call for beading, lace, studs, etc.?

Color palette
A color theme has a huge impact on a design or collection of designs. How many colors do you want to include? Brights, darks, pastels? Do they all work together? Are they tonal or contrasting? Try arranging colored squares of paper together or form them digitally to achieve your palette.

When finalizing a design

Positioning
How do your designs look from alternative angles? Try the side, front, back, tilted, straight, etc. Consider the effects of symmetry vs. asymmetry here too.

Function
Is it fit for purpose? The hat won't be successful if it is uncomfortable, too heavy, too wide for doors, blows off easily in the wind, too hot, etc. Try your designs on your head after every adjustment and keep in mind where they will be worn.

Design development exercise
This design exercise is intended as a warm-up, exploring the possibilities of a simple form of inspiration and incorporating it into hat shapes and trims, which can then be further refined into more-detailed designs. However, it's by no means the only way to explore your ideas.

Draw ten heads in any angles you wish.

Choose an object that inspires you or is related to a theme you like. I've used a basic square here.

Considering the first five design elements listed above (balance, shape, harmony, repetition, and scale), play with ways of using your object, or part of your object, on the heads. Try sketching ten in fifteen minutes. The timing is short in order to generate lots of ideas quickly.

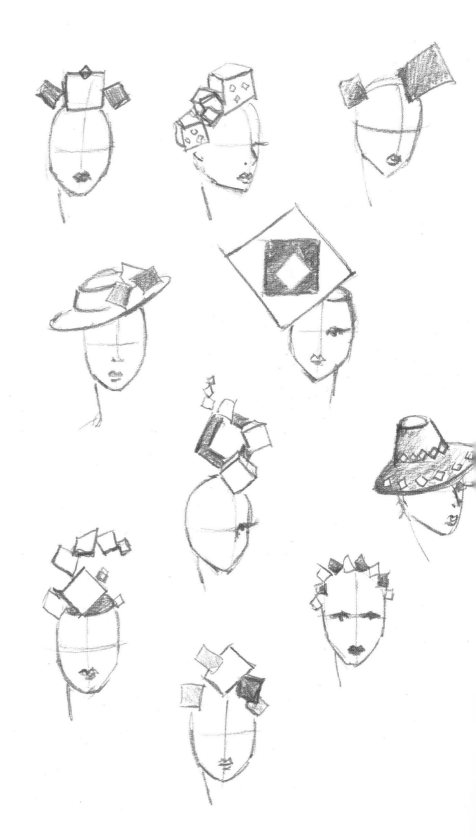

Now draw another five or so and try mixing in an additional element or two. Here I've incorporated rods. Spend some time considering further details for these, such as texture, color, position, and function. You could develop some of the first sketches, mix them up, and create new ones. Try using paints, pencils, pens, etc. to add color and texture.

Once you've jotted them down, look over them to see if you prefer some over others, or perhaps details that you may want to swap, accentuate, or remove.

You could try this again after researching a theme in depth, pulling together multiple elements of inspiration.

Designing for the Individual

If you are creating a design for a specific person, here are a few extra things worth considering.

Personality

Consider the characteristics of the individual. Is the wearer wanting to attract or deflect attention? Are they looking for something subtle or flamboyant? Do they suit a vibrant or muted color palette?

Personal tastes

They may have their own ideas that need incorporating, or an outfit or accessory that needs complementing in color, shape, and pattern.

Complexion and hair

Always check your intended color scheme against a person's own skin tone and hair color to make sure they complement each other. Colors that match too closely can look odd or lost or leave a person looking washed out. It has been a formal tradition to wear a hat slanted to the right, but complementing the wearer's own features such as sitting it on a side hair parting is more important.

Silhouette

If the wearer is tall, they can wear most shapes; however, overly high trims will stand out in a crowd, which may or may not be a good thing.

A shorter figure can end up hidden under a wide brim, so smaller widths or brim-free hats tend to work better. Slanting brims can also help.

Petite figures can carry small headpieces well, whereas fuller figures can carry larger hats better.

Environment and practicality

What type of event will it be worn at? Do weather conditions need to be taken into account? Will it be very busy or will they be greeting lots of people? Will it call for frivolity or formality? Hats with overly wide brims or trims can cause issues with practicality, so a smaller, slanted brim or trim may work better. Will they be moving around a lot or getting in and out of cars? If so, they may need a lighter or smaller hat with additional head attachments.

Budget

If somebody is paying for their hat, their budget may affect your material choices as well as the time you will be able to spend on the hat.

Face shape

Slanted angles are generally the most flattering, since their lines sit softer against the features. Other shapes and details vary according to face shape, as outlined on the opposite page.

Glasses

Wear hats away from the face, not too low on the forehead.

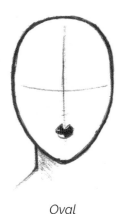

Oval

Oval/Heart

Most styles suit this shape. Wear straight or slanted; however, slanted gives a more even effect to the varying widths of the face. If the hat is brimless or has a small brim, the crown looks best if it is wider than the cheekbones/forehead.

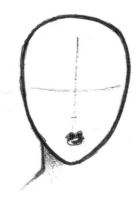

Heart

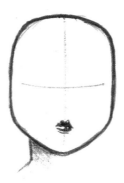

Square

Wear slanted or tilted, asymmetrical designs, curved lines, big brims.

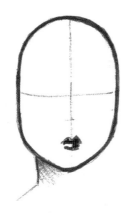

Long

Wear slanted, tilted, or straight. Brims and full hats are more complementary than tall, thinner shapes. Crowns that sit lower on the forehead suit this shape.

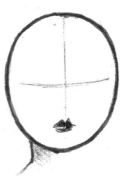

Round

Wear slanted styles or wide-brimmed hats that are asymmetrical. Avoid hats that sit low on the forehead.

Pattern Library

Here you'll find the patterns required for some of the projects throughout the book.

Each pattern is shown to scale; however, some will need to be enlarged to their specified size, with each square on the grid eventually measuring $\frac{2}{5}$" (1 cm). I recommend doing this by enlarging and copying on a photocopier. If that's not possible, they can be copied by hand by enlarging the grids and drawing the shapes on top, although this is less accurate.

Some patterns are bigger than a piece of A4 paper. If you don't have access to a large photocopier, copy the pattern in sections and stick them together. The pink lines indicate the half point and are there for guidance if you need to do this.

Transfer the CB and CF markings onto your material in removable chalk or pencil, since this will act as a guide when putting the pieces together.

If you think you may use the pattern more than once, it is a good idea to transfer it to card. This makes it more robust, and patterns can be drawn around and transferred onto fabric easier than in paper.

PATTERN SYMBOLS

Grain lines: Align the straight threads of the fabric (the warp and weft) parallel with the arrows, to ensure the correct incorporation of the bias.

Fold lines: The material will need to be folded at these lines at some point during construction.

CF: Center front of the pattern

CB: Center back of the pattern

Wire join: This indicates the location that is most discreet for wire joins.

Indicates where a pattern edge finishes or will be joined through sewing by hand or machine. The seam allowance is the extra material around the pattern, usually $\frac{2}{5}$" (1 cm).

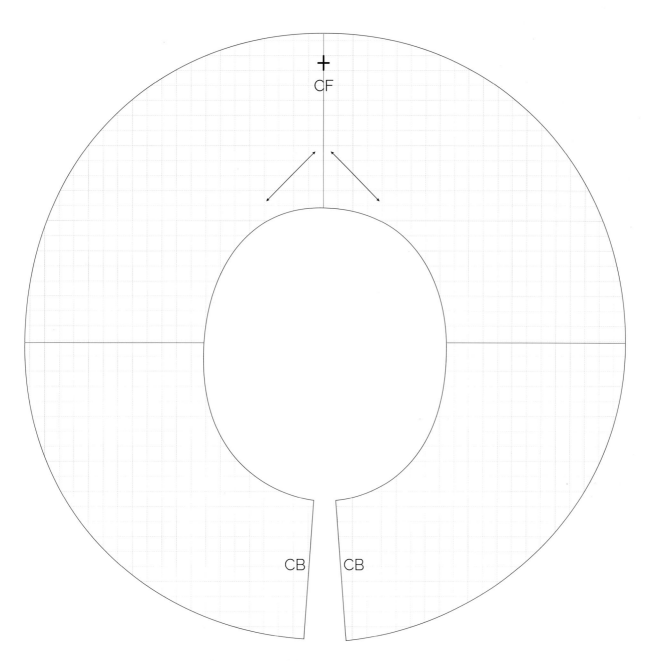

CF

CB   CB

Fabric-Covered Wide-Brim Boater—brim resize 250%

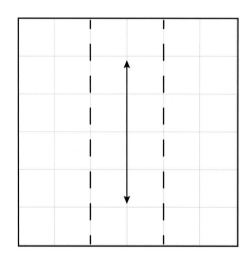

Fabric-Covered Wide-Brim Boater—bow loop at 100%

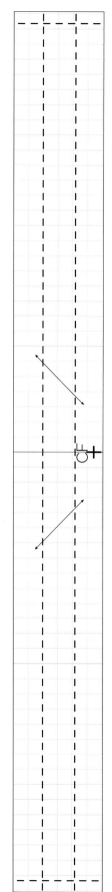

Fabric-Covered Wide-Brim Boater—hatband resize 250%

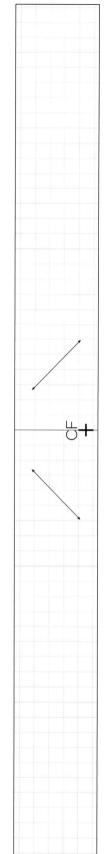

Fabric-Covered Wide-Brim Boater—side band resize 250%

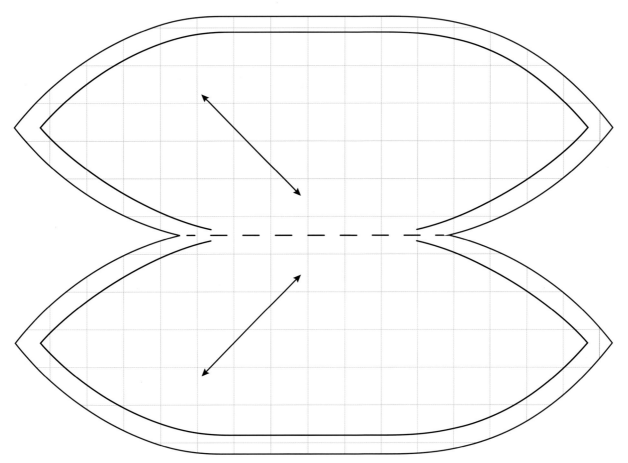

Fabric-Covered Wide-Brim Boater—bow at 100%

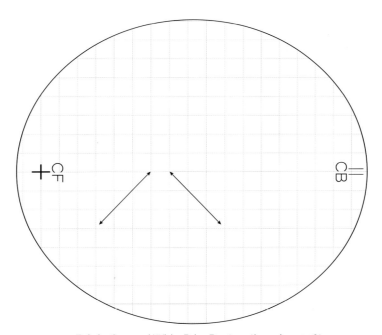

Fabric-Covered Wide-Brim Boater—tip resize 200%

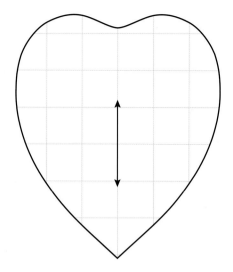

Versatile Rose—large-petal at 100%

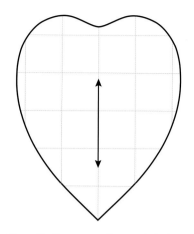

Versatile Rose—medium-petal at 100%

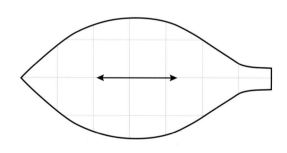

Versatile Rose—large-leaf at 100%

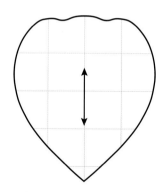

Versatile Rose—small-petal at 100%

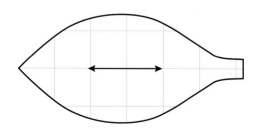

Versatile Rose—small-leaf at 100%

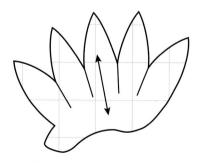

Versatile Rose—calyx at 100%

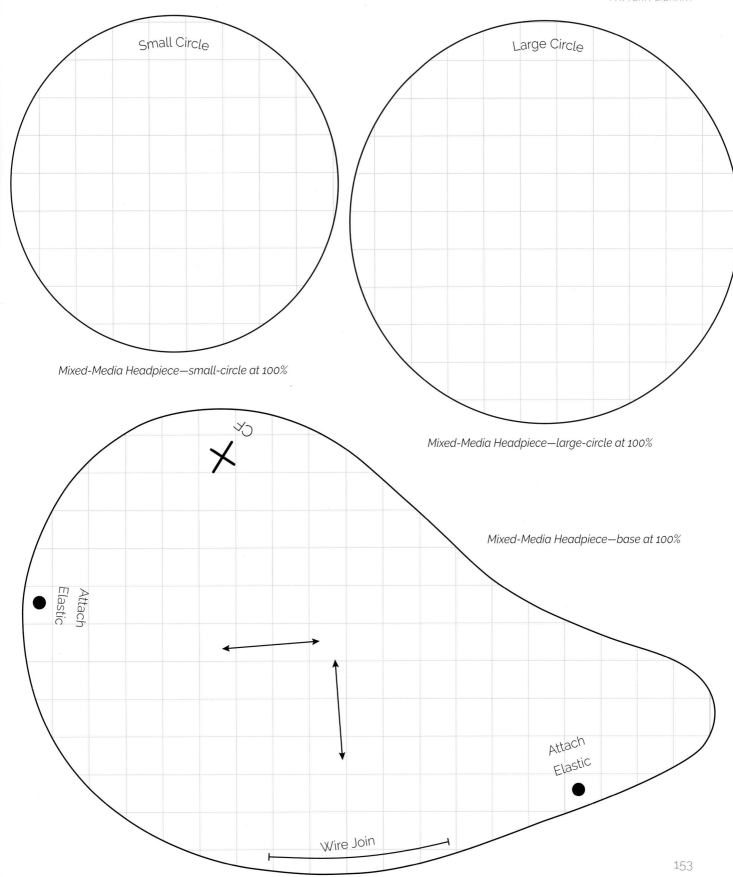

Small Circle

Large Circle

Mixed-Media Headpiece—small-circle at 100%

Mixed-Media Headpiece—large-circle at 100%

Mixed-Media Headpiece—base at 100%

CF

Attach
Elastic

Attach
Elastic

Wire Join

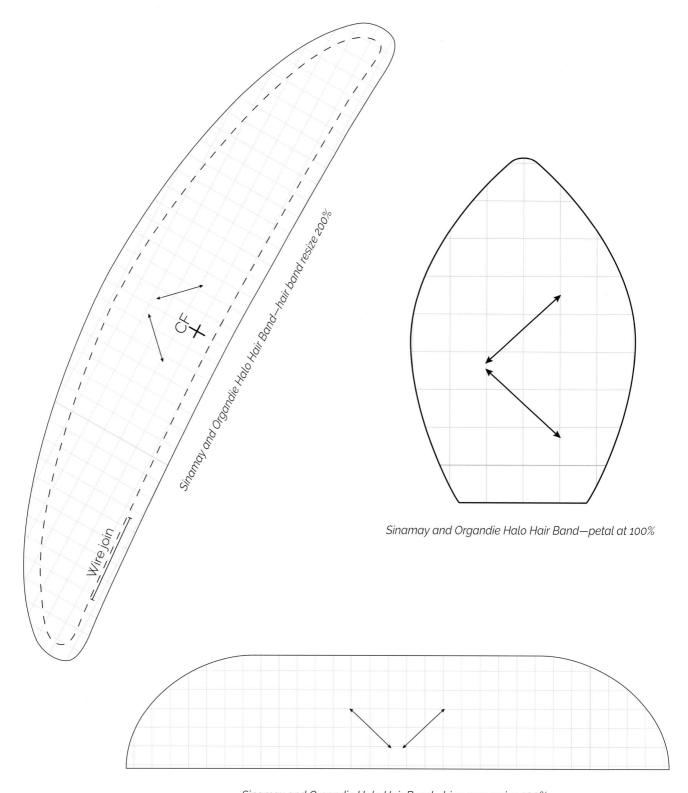

CF

Wire join

Sinamay and Organdie Halo Hair Band—hair band resize 200%

Sinamay and Organdie Halo Hair Band—petal at 100%

Sinamay and Organdie Halo Hair Band—bias rose resize 200%

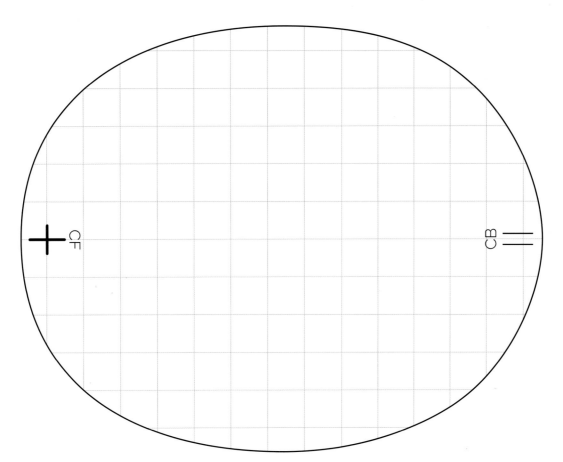

Patchwork Felt Pillbox—tip at 100%

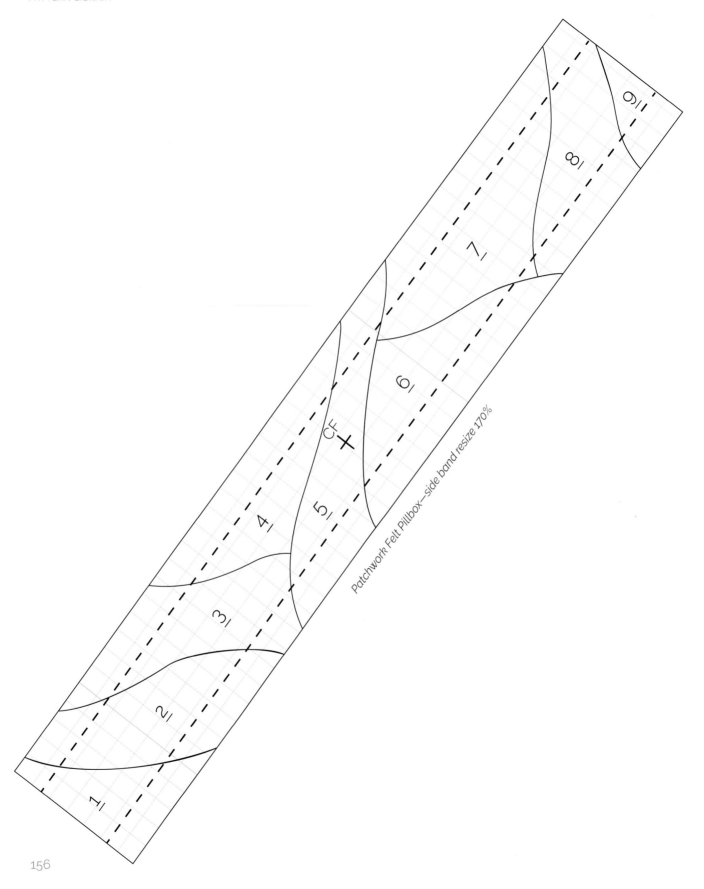

Patchwork Felt Pillbox—side band resize 170%

CF

1
2
3
4
5
6
7
8
9

Troubleshooting

Dented or misshapen blocked hats
Iron with a damp cloth on the area to soften it, then remold and hold with your fingers. You may also need more stiffener.

Blocked shape is too soft
Add more stiffener to the affected areas.

Stiffener residue
Apply hairspray, thinners, or more stiffener, dependent on the type. Stiffener can be removed from sinamay with a pin.

Distorted brim
Wire may be too big or too small.

Felt slightly too small for block
Soak the felt or thoroughly wet and steam with a cloth and iron, then pull with pliers.

Creases on underside of blocked felt
Use a wire brush or toothbrush on the fibers, or scratch a pin over the area.

Pin marks left in material after blocking
Scratch over with a pin on felt, or move fibers carefully with a pin on straw, fabric, and sinamay.

Dirty marks
Remove by repeatedly sticking and peeling off sticky tape. Wet wipes are also effective.

Run out of thread midstitch
Finish the thread with a knot under a fold or behind something and start again, hiding the new knot in the same way.

Thread keeps knotting/snapping
Keep thread short—never longer than arm's length. Run it through beeswax if it's knotted or weak. Make sure the thread doesn't rub against the thimble you're when sewing.

Visible stitches
Use a pen to carefully color them the same color as the hat, or if on felt, try brushing the felt over them.

Buckram under blocked fabric/leather is buckling
Fabric may be pulled too tight; you may need an additional layer of buckram for strength or an extra wire support.

Sinamay/straw corners or folds are brittle and fraying
Dampen the material before folding/rolling. Add stiffener to the area and iron to seal once dry.

Needle is difficult to pull through hat
Pull the needle with flat-nosed pliers.

List of Suppliers and Useful Links

This list is here to get you started but is by no means exhaustive; there may be other suppliers more local to you.

General millinery supplies

Artipistilos (Spain)
www.artipistilos.com

Baxter Hart & Abraham Ltd. (UK)
www.baxterhart.co.uk

De Vroey bvba (Belgium)
www.devroeyhats.be

Gennaro Gori (Italy)
www.gennarogorispa.com

Hats by Leko (USA)
www.hatsupply.com

Hatters Millinery Supplies (Australia)
www.hattersmillinerysupplies.com.au

House of Adorn (Australia)
www.houseofadorn.com

Judith M Inc. (USA)
www.judithm.com

MacCulloch and Wallis Ltd. (UK)
www.macculloch-wallis.co.uk

Parkin (UK)
www.parkinfabrics.co.uk

Petershams Millinery Supplies (UK)
www.petershams.com

Pierre & Pierre Millinery Supplies (Netherlands)
www.pierre-et-pierre.net

Plooij Hats & Materials bv (Netherlands)
www.plooij.nu

Millinery Hub (formerly Torb & Reiner) (Australia)
www.millineryhub.com.au

Hat blocks

Boon & Lane Ltd. (UK)
www.hatblockstore.co.uk

Easy Hat Blocks (Latvia)
www.easyhatblocks.com

Guy Morse-Brown (UK)
www.hatblocks.co.uk

Hat Blocks Australia (Australia)
www.hatblocksaustralia.com.au

The Hat Block Library (UK)
www.hatblock.co.uk
(Hat block hire)

Feathers

Dersh Feathers (USA)
www.dershfeather.com

Feather Place (USA)
www.featherplace.com

Ostrich Feather Manufacturing Co. Ltd. (UK)
www.ostrichfeather.co.uk

The Feather Factory (UK)
www.thefeatherfactory.co.uk

Jaffé Feathers (UK)
www.jaffefeathers.co.uk

Useful links

Hat Magazine
www.thehatmagazine.com

The British Hat Guild
www.thebritishhatguild.org.uk

The British Millinery Association
www.britishmilleryassociation.com

The Millinery Association of Australia
www.millineryaustralia.org

The USA Milliners Guild
www.millinersguild.org

The Dutch Hats Association (NHV)
www.nederlandsehoedenvereniging.com

Asociacion de Sombrereros (Spanish Millinery Society)
www.asociacionespanoladesombureria.com

Techniques Index

About the Author

Multi-award-winning milliner, designer, and tutor Sophie Beale developed her unique blend of knowledge working in some of London's finest couture millinery workrooms, where she made hats for many celebrities and fashion houses, having previously studied HNC Millinery at world-renowned Kensington and Chelsea College, and with Royal Milliner Rose Cory and respected Milliner Hilary Peach.

With a wide-ranging knowledge of millinery and a degree in costume design, Sophie Beale teaches her craft within the UK and internationally. Her hats have been exhibited at London and Paris Fashion week, among Europe's finest artisans at Homo Faber Venice, and within a permanent display at the National Museum of Scotland. Her work has appeared on television programs, on the cover of the Royal Ascot style guide, and as part of the official "Ascot Millinery Collective."

Once named "Britain's hottest new milliner" by the British Fashion Council and *Grazia Magazine,* Sophie creates conceptual, innovative, and flattering headpieces. She is a founder member of the British Hat Guild and regularly designs the "inspiration" pages for the industry's *Hat Magazine.*

www.sophiebealemillinery.com